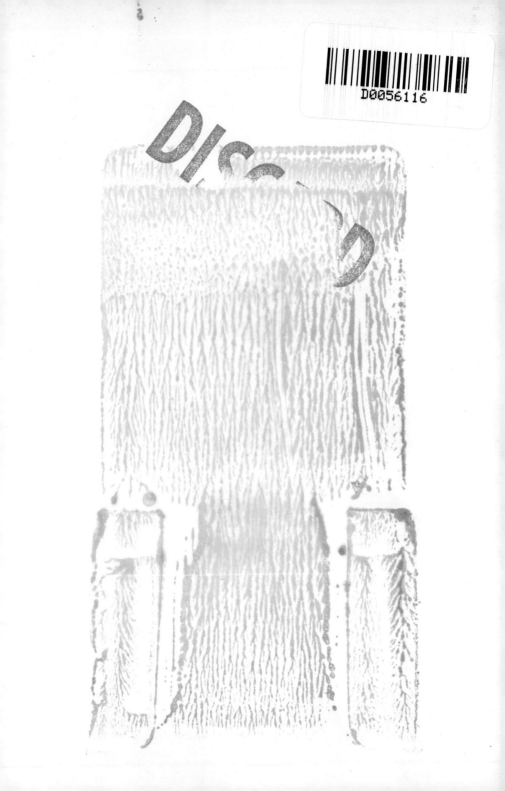

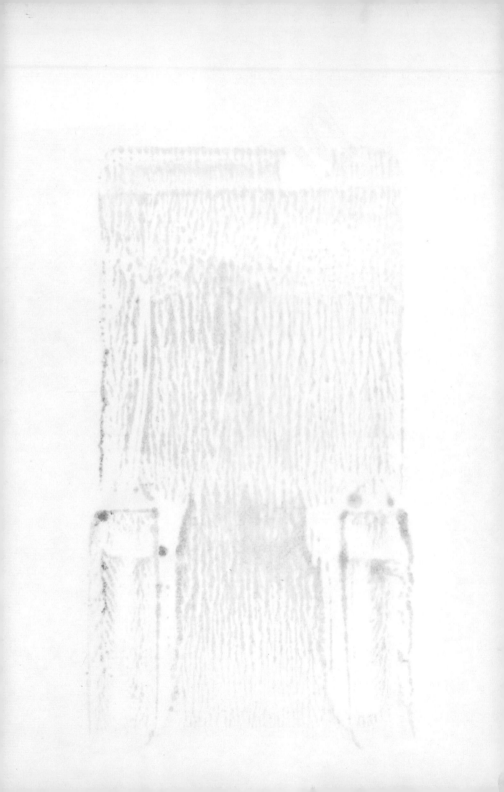

How to Teach Your Students to Write

HOW TO TEACH YOUR STUDENTS TO WRITE / *A Guide*

to Creative Writing for Teaching and Self-Study

by CATHERINE LINDSAY

Funk & Wagnalls / New York

Published by Funk & Wagnalls, *A Division of*
Reader's Digest Books, Inc.

Printed in the United States of America

How to Teach Your Students to Write

I

Why This Book Was Written

Some years ago, in September of 1949 to be exact, I stood before a class of college students who solemnly expected to be taught to write. Although I had received my B.A. and my M.A. degrees from a reputable Midwestern university, and although I had published by then a well-reviewed short novel, no one anywhere had prepared me to "teach" writing. There were no books to guide me—and I examined many; there was no syllabus issued by the university in whose halls I stood that September afternoon, no advice from my department chairman, and no diagrams or lesson plans which I myself had prepared—how could I?

I began that first class, I remember, by reading aloud the first chapter of Ernest Hemingway's *A Farewell to Arms*. The class listened. When I had finished reading the two or three hundred lines, I asked those solemn, quiet, ungiving, and, to me, rather frightening faces why they thought—if they did—Hemingway's words were "good writing." I wrote a single sentence on the blackboard: What are the elements of good writing?

And waited.

There was no response.

I read the chapter again, more slowly and more carefully, stressing the variety in the sentence structure, the alliteration, the symbolism, the contrasts. Silence again. At last a hand was raised; one of the students spoke, answering the question which stared back from the long blackboard. Another hand went up; I listened to another answer.

At the end of that first class session I had accomplished something almost by accident. I had gotten those unknown students to talk and to think about writing. The next step, of course, was to get them to write. But to write what? To learn how slowly? How quickly? To use how many models and whose? Dickens? Faulkner? Churchill? Ernie Pyle? And how to keep them writing when their first efforts were unorganized (and they were) clichés?

The teaching of writing, I am convinced, is learned by the teacher while he is teaching, since teaching is an art form like any other. However, there are certain tricks and certain programs which seem to work, which do make the college student, adult or near-adult, write and learn to write. Most textbooks on writing are anthologies of the works of successful writers. Sometimes the editors append questions about the writing, questions designed to make the student create his own imitations. But imitations are not expressive learning, and they are not writing, any more than a photograph of a painting or a free-hand, copied drawing are original or meaningful works.

The teacher of writing cannot proceed only by means of his zeal and good will. The textbooks containing model selections will not help the student. It is to fill, as much as possible, the need of a program for the teacher, as well as to give a program to the student, one that will not frustrate nor drown his capacity and material, that this small book was written.

II

The First Class Session:
What Is "Good Writing"?

A group of student writers is as polyglot and therefore as interesting as any group anywhere, reflecting as it does every sort of age, occupation, and skill, every sort of educational background (in an adult class), and, above all, reflecting a kind of restlessness, a dissatisfaction with ordinary life, and a confidence beyond the ordinary. Each student is in the class because he believes he has some comment to make about the world he is in. And each student feels he can make that comment only with guidance and help. He is not yet a writer, or he would be, clearly, sitting before his typewriter already writing. He may have several rejected manuscripts in his desk at his office, in a bureau drawer at his apartment—or he may have none at all. But he comes to the class already interested, and he is in the class because he recognizes his need for help.

7

And he values his own life experience or he would not want to write about it.

These are the plus factors which not only the student but the teacher have to work with. Essentially, both teacher and student are faced with the challenge of turning a vague desire "to write" into disciplined production in a special form—the short story, the essay, the book review, the novel, perhaps even the cookbook. The student needs specific criticism, of course, but he needs to learn form, and he must find the form for which his own talent and energy are suited.

But first of all he has to understand what writing—good writing—means. He must understand that it contains elements which he can learn and which he must learn in order to use them, to make his own writing "good."

After twenty years of teaching writing classes in which most (not all, it will never be all) of my students learned to write, I have not found a substitute for that first, long-ago session at that Midwestern university brave enough to hire a teacher of writing who had had no experience of teaching. The first class session has been and will continue to be, as long as it proves successful, an attempt to make the students think of answers to the blackboard question: What are the elements of good writing?

After a ten-minute period in which each student should be asked to introduce himself and give to the class as well as to the teacher some brief account of his writing experience, the teacher can do no better than to write the all-important question on the blackboard. And the teacher can do no better than to read two selections that quickly illustrate the answers the students themselves must give.

A Farewell to Arms is easily obtainable. Its use as a whole book illustrating character, contrast, symbolism, and direct statement of theme will be discussed later. However, it might save time to quote its first chapter here. The second selection, the first page and a half of Isak Dinesen's *Out of Africa,* will be quoted because, unlike the Hemingway novel, it is sometimes out of print.

The class then at its first session announces itself, speaks of its writing background and perhaps of its reasons for taking a writing course. The important question has been written in bold letters on the blackboard. The teacher, with trembling hands or not, depending upon his own confidence and experience, opens his text and reads—slowly; Hemingway has become the teacher, for the time being:

> In the late summer of that year we lived in a house in a village that looked across the river and the plain to the mountains. In the bed of the river there were pebbles and boulders, dry and white in the sun, and the water was clear and swiftly moving and blue in the channels. Troops went by the house and down the road and the dust they raised powdered the leaves of the trees. The trunks of the trees too were dusty and the leaves fell early that year and we saw the troops marching along the road and the dust rising and leaves, stirred by the breeze, falling and the soldiers marching and afterward the road bare and white except for the leaves.

Although this is not the end of the selection, the teacher might do well to pause here before continuing. The first class is, after all, the first class, and the students may be as disoriented, as uneasy as the teacher himself and they may not be prepared to listen for long periods. Also they may need prodding. It is effective to reread this passage stressing, of course, the *l*'s. (The first two sentences are fraught with the letter *l*.) The teacher might ask why the sentences are rhythmical and what glues them together. Is there any repeated

9

sound? Reading these first sentences again will emphasize this for the students. Hands will go up.

One more interruption will be useful here. The teacher, in reading, might draw on the board long and short lines to correspond with the sentences' lengths as they are read. This too will emphasize a reason for their rhythm; the sentences are not of equal length. They will look on the blackboard something like _____. _____, and _____, _____. _____. The students will comment on this. There will be two answers at once to the blackboard question, What are the elements of good writing? The answers, of course, will be: variety in sentence length and the repetition of a letter sound—in this case, *l*.

And the teacher will continue to read the short selection:

The plain was rich with crops; there were many orchards of fruit trees and beyond the plain the mountains were brown and bare. There was fighting in the mountains and at night we could see the flashes from the artillery. In the dark it was like summer lightning, but the nights were cool and there was not the feeling of a storm coming.

Sometimes in the dark we heard the troops marching under the windows and guns going past pulled by motor tractors. There was much traffic at night and many mules on the roads with boxes of ammunition on each side of their pack-saddles and gray motor trucks that carried men, and other trucks with loads covered with canvas that moved slower in the traffic. There were big guns too that passed in the day drawn by tractors, the long barrels of the guns covered with green branches and green leafy branches and vines laid over the tractors. To the north we could look across a valley and see a forest of chestnut trees and behind it another mountain on this side of the river. There was fighting for that mountain, too, but it was not successful, and in the fall when the rains came the leaves all fell from the chestnut trees and the branches were bare and the trunks black with rain. The vineyards were thin and bare-branched too and all the country wet and brown with the autumn. There were mists over the river and clouds on the mountain and the trucks splashed mud on the road and the troops were muddy and wet in their capes; their rifles were wet and under their capes the two leather cartridge-boxes on the front of the belts, gray leather boxes heavy with the packs of clips of thin, long 6.5 mm. cartridges, bulged forward under the capes so that the men, passing on the road, marched as though they were six months gone with child.

There were small gray motor cars that passed going very fast; usually there was an officer on the seat with the driver and more officers in the back seat. They splashed more mud than the camions even and if one of the officers in the back was very small and sitting between two generals, he himself so small that you could not see his face but only the top of his cap and his narrow back, and if the car went especially fast it was probably the King. He lived in Udine and came out in this way nearly every day to see how things were going, and things went very badly.

At the start of the winter came the permanent rain and with the rain came the cholera. But it was checked and in the end only seven thousand died of it in the army.

This is, of course, eminently good writing. But why? The blackboard question has been partly answered: variety in sentence length, repetition of sounds. But what else?

It is here that a bit of explication is useful. Hemingway, after all, was only in his late twenties when *A Farewell to Arms* was published. This fact is an encouragement to the rows of faces and should be mentioned. The novel is an account of his own experience as a volunteer ambulance driver in the Italian Army, as a wounded soldier, as a lover, and as someone whose education, in relation to life-as-tragedy, was completed by this experience. But what makes this writing "good writing"?

For one thing, is there irony in the chapter? (The teacher should make certain that the meaning of irony as both understatement and symbol is clear to the class.) Where is the irony? For whom was the war fought? For a king shorter in stature than any of his officers, a figure whose ineffectuality is clear when we read that he only came out to "see" how things were going. Things were going badly, but the king could not change them. Is irony then an element of good writing? Does an ironical answer to a question about one's health on a hot New York summer afternoon, for example, after subway crowds, noise, and an office filled with unending paperwork a question answered by, "Never better; I expect to run for mayor next week"—is this statement more effective than, "I'm all right. No complaints"? Well, of course it is.

And there are other examples of irony in the selection. What about the fact that only seven thousand died of cholera in the army? How is this irony—an element of good writing as it is—an effective comment on war, a world war in which 8,500,000 men died in action? And what about the fact that the men marching with cartridges bulging beneath their raincapes looked like pregnant women—were, in other words, deformed, unsexed by the war? An irony? Of course.

Is there symbolism in the selection? And what is "symbolism"? It is necessary for a teacher of anything—cookery, quantum physics, or karate—to define his terms. One might say that symbolism is a specific object (like a flag, a wedding ring, a robin) standing for an abstraction, an idea (like country, marriage, or spring). Symbolism is the meat of writers. And it is sometimes the bread and the wine as well, because a symbol is a kind of shorthand; it can say much in little. Well, the teacher might say to the class, since symbolism is an element of good writing, we might expect Hemingway to use it. Does he?

The class will answer—if the teacher has made symbolism real to them with everyday examples. Does Hemingway use symbolism in this brief chapter? What about the mud that dirties and corrodes both men and machines? What about the leaves, repeated so often that they are clearly a symbol? Isn't Hemingway saying that the men were falling like the autumn leaves and as anonymously? Even the autumn itself is emphasized, the death of the year, as a symbol of that death which marches with the men along the dusty roads.

But what about contrast? Contrast, after all, is an element used in music, in painting, in cookery, and in house and dress design among other things. An interior decorator will use color contrasts, line contrasts, and texture contrasts to bring out the element of color, shape, and texture. How does Hemingway use contrast here?

In the beginning of the selection the river is described as being clear, so clear that its pebbles are white in the sun. Later, the river is muddied by the dust from the marching feet; the trees are stripped to provide camouflage for the guns; the sky is unnaturally lighted by flashes from the artillery. Nature itself is overcome by the energy of war; it is brutalized and changed.

The class now ought to be ready to list some of the elements of good writing in their notebooks, to be reviewed and used when they began to write. And these are:

1. Repetition of letter sounds
2. Variety in sentence length
3. Irony
4. Symbolism
5. Contrast

Perhaps this will be enough for the first session. A teacher's "plan" must always be loose since the point of teaching is cardinally not to impose a plan but only to use a plan to make the students come alive, to make them work and think. The teacher of writing who faces his or her first class has accomplished enough for one day if that class has come to think about what good writing is.

III

Session Two:
What Shall I Write?

A university class is usually scheduled to meet for a fifty-minute period, two or three times a week. Occasionally, a class is scheduled to meet for a longer, two-hour period once a week. If this latter is true, the instructor can combine the two selections (Hemingway and Dinesen) mentioned in Chapter I. The question on the board will be the same, What are the elements of good writing? And the advantage of a longer session is, of course, that the interest created by the teacher, by the selections, and by the class response can be maintained.

If the second class meeting should occur after a period of days, the teacher will do well to review the answers to the all-important blackboard question that were given in the first class session. And it might be well to announce that the second session, or the third, as the case may be, is the time for the first assignment, the first piece of good writing.

As always, in reading a selection for class comment, some mention of the writer's background is relevant and valuable. Isak Dinesen, in writing *Out of Africa*, was writing from her own experience, the experience of establishing and managing a coffee plantation in the highlands of Kenya, near Nairobi. In the years before her plantation failed, Baroness Blixen (her pen name is taken from her Danish maiden name, Dinesen) had a passionate and enduring love affair with Africa. Her book, therefore, is a factual account. She is writing, as all writers must write, from what she knows; she is writing firsthand.

But she is using, as the teacher can remind the class, the same tricks, the same elements that Hemingway used:

I had a farm in Africa, at the foot of the Ngong Hills. The Equator runs across these highlands, a hundred miles to the North, and the farm lay at an altitude of over six thousand feet. In the day-time you felt that you had got high up, near to the sun, but the early mornings and evenings were limpid and restful, and the nights were cold.

It might be a good idea to pause here to ask the students what elements of good writing are again used. Variety in sentence length is clear. The teacher might read the first sentences again and at the same time measure their length by lines drawn on the board. And what about the repetition of the letter sound *h?* And of the *l* sound again? Combined, of course, they take the listener *up,* as the teacher, speaking an *h* and then an *l,* can demonstrate.

The geographical position, and the height of the land combined to create a landscape that had not its like in all the world. [The *l* sound again!] There was no fat on it and no luxuriance anywhere; it was Africa distilled up through six thousand feet, like the strong and refined essence of a continent. The colours were dry and burnt, like the colours in pottery. The trees had a light, delicate foliage, the structure of which was different from that of the trees in Europe; it did not grow in bows or cupolas, but in horizontal layers, and the formation gave to the tall, solitary trees a likeness to the palms, or a heroic and romantic air like fullrigged ships with their sails clewed up,

(Here, in order to clarify the simile, the teacher might draw on the board a picture of a sailing ship with horizontal cross masts and furled sails—and beside it a picture of trees growing in layers, horizontal rather than vertical.)

and to the edge of a wood a strange appearance as if the whole wood were faintly vibrating. Upon the grass of the great plains the crooked bare old thorn-trees were scattered, and the grass was spiced like thyme and bog-myrtle; in some places the scent was so strong that it smarted in the nostrils. All the flowers that you found on the plains, or upon the creepers and liana in the native forest were diminutive like flowers of the downs,—only just in the beginning of the long rains a number of big, massive, heavy-scented lilies sprang out on the plains. The views were immensely wide. Everything that you saw made for greatness and freedom, and unequalled nobility.

The chief feature of the landscape, and of your life in it, was the air. Looking back on a sojourn in the African highlands, you are struck by your feeling of having lived for a time up in the air. The sky was rarely more than pale blue or violet, with a profusion of mighty, weightless, ever-changing clouds towering up and sailing on it, but it had a blue vigour in it, and at a short distance it painted the ranges of the hills and the woods a fresh deep blue. In the middle of the day the air was alive over the land, like a flame burning; it scintillated, waved, and shone like running water. . . .

17

What are the elements of good writing? What does this passage contain that Hemingway's chapter did not? What in the reader is appealed to, brought forth, that Hemingway did not appeal to nor bring forth? What comparisons are made and how is the writing made effective by them?

In relation to the third question, the alert student, or even the not-so-alert, will mention that the *senses* of the reader are appealed to. And this will give the teacher a valuable opportunity to point out that the beginning writer often forgets that his reader is more than visual. Dinesen reminds the reader that he can smell ("the grass was spiced like thyme and bog-myrtle") and that he can feel in a kinesthetic sense ("you are struck by your feeling of having lived for a time up in the air").

The reader, the teacher might say, has five senses and not just one. The reader can feel, taste, smell, and touch as well as see. All good writers know this; all bad writers forget it. Only the bad writer describes a scene in solely visual terms.

So, what are the elements of good writing not yet mentioned? The class will answer: An appeal to the reader's five senses.

And what else?

What about Dinesen's comparisons? The land, she says, has no fat on it. Isn't this a comparison of a country and a person? And isn't one thing compared with another stronger because of the comparison? Isn't a man described as being as tall as Lincoln taller than simply a tall man? And isn't a child as intelligent as David Copperfield clearly more than just an intelligent child? And isn't a fat lady, as fat as Baby Ruth (of American circus fame), fatter than just a lady whose fat does not and cannot connote the same rolls, winnows, and myriad chins? Comparison is another of the elements of good writing.

But they must be fresh. Dead as a dog, blue as the sky, bright as a dollar, no longer connote anything to anyone. Metaphors or similes have got to have something of the writer in them, some of his own discoveries, in order to move and delight the reader, in order to surprise him. Who, for example, except a good writer could compare an African tree with a sailing ship? Or the colors of Africa with the dry, earthy colors of pottery?

Again, What are the elements of good writing?

1. Comparisons, but fresh comparisons
2. An appeal to the reader's five senses

And, to review,

3. Variety in sentence length
4. Repetition of letter sounds
5. Irony
6. Symbolism
7. Contrast
8. And a subject that the writer knows well

Perhaps this is the time to end Session Two (or the second half of Session One). The writing assignment is a description of a place, one that the student knows well.

And this assignment ought to be written in class, during the second or third class meeting. It should be outlined before the class meets—that is, the writer should list the elements of good writing which he intends to employ as well as the details he will use in his description. But the writing itself should be done in the class period—because any teacher is aware that a well-motivated class (horrible as that expression may be) is sometimes over-motivated; it will cheat. And any teacher also knows that writing ought not to be a chore. In an outside assignment a studious (often neurotic) student

19

may produce a description representing forty or fifty hours of hard work, while another will write his in twenty minutes. A class assignment in the beginning, while unifying the group, will obviate these two extremes.

But a good teacher will talk about the assignment. What, for example, is a place where you (the student writer) felt changed, harmed, or helped? Was it your first job? Your wedding day? Your first visit to the income tax department, when you were prepared for self-defense? Your first bank loan? Your first social victory? What was it like? How did it look, smell, feel, taste (even fear has a taste), sound?

This, then, is assignment one. The class will come to the next session prepared to write. The elements of good writing, elements the class itself has named and discussed, will be listed on the board. The assignment will be no more than a two-page paper, but it will be "motivated" in that the students will be expressing themselves and will be using the same elements used by other writers. However, they will not be imitating these writers nor awed by them.

IV

Session Three (or Four):
What Should the Teacher Say?

It is a dour, unrelated, unwilling, and unfeeling human being who can wait passively while his class of students stir, think, grimace, and create in a silent room before his eyes. If the teacher can survive such an hour without being moved or touched, even the most charitable adviser ought to tell him simply that he is in the wrong profession. Teaching is communication but is also, trite as it may seem, love.

One cares about these strangers' faces. Why? Perhaps because one had a loving grandmother whose hand stilled many crises and injustices, or because one wanted to do unto others as one was not done to in order to redress the balance, or because one had a teacher who "gave." A teacher is committed to humanity or he is not a teacher. If he does not groan, hope, smile, and yearn while his students work for him, and for themselves, he had best approach his chairman at the earliest opportunity to talk about another career. But since a dedication is a *sine qua non* for any profession, this book is written for those teachers who have it.

And so the students turn in their first themes. Smiling, nodding, and offering signs of pleasure, the teacher collects the papers. Blessed with a motor car, or condemned to a subway, he carries the papers home. He dines. He walks. He returns to his room, apartment, house, or hovel. He reads the papers.

He is despondent.

Why is he despondent?

He is despondent because the papers are so bad.

Why are the papers so bad?

They are so bad because the students can't write.

The teacher has a drink. Or a pot of coffee. Perhaps he walks again or lies on his bed with his forearm sheltering his eyes and thinks of Greek isles, Tahitian sunsets, the Peace Corps, advertising jobs as listed in *The New York Times,* his maiden aunt who offers a large house with a room "to write in" overlooking the garden.

Well. What, after rousing himself to read the papers again, does the teacher find?

He finds clichés, bad spelling, impossible punctuation, horrible grammar, egocentric logic, and never a "seed beneath the snow," never a sentence containing any indication that "the corn is green."

What does he do? To correct the errors is a labor of Hercules. Better, he thinks—after hours of marking comma splices, misspellings, *non sequiturs*—better to give up the whole lot, to start the class again.

He's right.

And so he approaches, papers under his unsteady arm, Session Number Four, which—having approached it before— one might call the moment of truth.

22

V

Cold Turkey:
The First Paper

To describe, portray, or otherwise indicate the effect of a teacher upon a writing class, a teacher loaded with first papers and a writing class already waiting to interpret criticism as misunderstanding, is a chapter of a novel as yet unwritten. The teacher approaches it; the class waits.

The papers are terrible. Even the more or less readable papers are terrible because they indicate no knowledge of spelling or punctuation.

What does the teacher do?

He lists ten punctuation rules clearly on the board and explains each. He lists common clichés (having copied them from all the papers), and asks the class to turn in their own lists of clichés at the next session.

He reminds the class of the elements of good writing, few of which were used in paper number one. He assigns another paper on the same subject, a description of place, to be written at home.

What are the punctuation rules?

I have "boiled them down" to ten. Textbooks expounding upon them can be found anywhere, but they also abort your plan to teach your students to write because the students become enmeshed in a net of commas. Some rules are necessary, but the fewer they can be made, the better. And the teacher might begin to "teach" them by speaking of punctuation marks as sign-posts; the comma, colon, semicolon, period, etc., are simply ways for the writer to tell the reader when to pause, stop, halfstop, break, or leap. The teacher should make this clear, proceed to the rules, give a short test several sessions later, and that is all.

And why are these rules necessarily emphasized in a college class where it should be assumed that they have been learned long ago? Because the public grade schools and high schools of the United States have been for years so crowded, so poorly staffed (teaching is secure!), so poisoned by ideas of permissiveness and democratic goals—whatever they are—that the average American college student will not really know anything requiring definition, facts, or logic.

He may not know what a comma is for, and he may have never used the dash or the parenthesis. Unless, therefore, he knows that a semicolon means a half stop, a period a full stop, and a colon a stop long enough to indicate that something is to follow, he cannot use even ten rules properly and will not be able to punctuate at all.

The teacher then writes these rules on the board. However, before he begins to show how they work, he had better make sure that his class knows what words like "sentence," "clause," "indirect object," and phrases like "dependent clause" and "predicate nominative" really mean. (A revision of the program of the American public school system may very well be in order, but meanwhile your writing class waits.)

These are the ten rules; the class will copy them into their notebooks:

1. A long, dependent clause out of order is set off by commas; a dependent clause in order is not set off by commas

2. Two or more independent clauses not joined by a coordinating conjunction are separated by a semicolon

3. Two or more independent clauses joined by a coordinating conjunction are separated by a comma before the conjunction

4. Quoted matter is set off from nonquoted matter by both commas and quotation marks

5. Names of ships, trains, planes, magazines, newspapers and books, foreign words and phrases, letters of the alphabet, and words in emphasis are underlined

6. A dash is used only to indicate a physical interruption or sudden change of thought

7. Parentheses are used to set off material that has no essential connection to the rest of the sentence

8. Brackets are used only to indicate the author's comment within a quotation

9. Colons are used to indicate material to follow, usually preceded by phrases like "as follows," or "the following," or "such as"

10. Nouns and phrases in apposition are set off by commas

This is a small list, but it will serve, and it may be the *only* list of punctuation rules your students have seen. The students, of course, should memorize it as soon as possible. A punctuation test, in which they write the rules and examples, ought to be given during the next class session. (It will help if you will announce beforehand that the test is "all or nothing"—students missing one rule will earn a zero. And all the written work of the semester should be corrected in relation to the rules, i.e., the missing or erroneous punctuation mark should be corrected and the rule written out.)

Clichés

We live in a world of signboards, television, portable radios, and permanent loudspeakers. Above all, we are barraged by advertising slogans from every newspaper and magazine we read, and every subway, streetcar, or bus upon which we travel. We live, in fact, within a world dedicated to the cliché, because the cliché sells. It is hardly surprising, therefore, to find student papers filled with little ease.

But there are remedies. The clichés listed by the teacher from the first papers, and already mentioned, can be read aloud. The weakness of the cliché (weak because it connotes the obvious, generalized image) can be discussed and emphasized. Each student, as was suggested, can be asked to hand in to the teacher a list of his own most-used clichés, those he hopes to exorcise from his own writing.

And the student papers can be read aloud—of course, only the best ones. It is always necessary for the teacher to remember that even a small piece of writing, especially creative writing, represents something very special and dear to the writer. A "bad" piece of student writing should *never* be read aloud to a class, no matter how well it may illustrate writing faults. A good piece of writing, on the other hand, should be praised first by the teacher, then by the other students (encouraged by the teacher to make comments) until the student writer, pleased with approbation, is ready to hear and see where he has erred, how many of his comparisons are not fresh, how few of the five senses he has appealed to, how many opportunities for contrast he has missed. Always the teacher need not have the patience of a saint, but he should have the instincts of a showman, or of a master of ceremonies. One does not attack a member of the audience; one encourages him.

The Interview

Nearly all college teachers, of writing or anything else, are given an office. This can be a desk, chair, and breathing space, or something more elaborate. But it is valuable only as it is used. It should not be used by the teacher simply to correct papers; it should be used to interview students about their papers as frequently as the papers and time permit. And a promising student deserves more time than a hopeless one. (The hopeless one, of course, deserves time too, perhaps more than any other student in the beginning of the semester; later it may be another story.)

What is the interview? It is first of all a student with a paper whose corrections and comments he cannot understand. Nine times out of ten he feels he has been "done in." He may be suffering from a neurotic feeling of superiority and hence of persecution, or from a series of bad, unfeeling, and incompetent teachers, or from general dull-wittedness, or from personal problems to which the paper he hopes can be an "Open Sesame" to Someone Who Understands. In each case, he deserves an early interview.

And the best possible approach on the part of the teacher, for all exigencies, is to reread the paper carefully aloud while the student listens to your comments.

27

Better teaching can be done in the interview (which is, in point of fact, a teaching session) than in a series of student papers, no matter how carefully marked with comments they might be. The student, after all, is in your office, a breathing, living, suffering student writer. And his creation is in your hands. You, after all, know the elements of good writing. Why hasn't he used them? Well, does he understand them? Does he know what a cliché is really? Does he care enough to learn to punctuate properly? Does he need encouragement (and most students do)?

The first interview is the teacher's chance to reemphasize the lessons of the first meetings, to chat in a friendly, face-to-face way with the student, above all, to interest him.

And if, as sometimes happens, the first paper shows no talent at all, no originality, no enthusiasm, do not say so. The first paper is only a beginning; perhaps the student will do better in later ones. And he will do better if the teacher does well in the interview, in face-to-face talk, and in a careful examination of what he has written. The first interview is really the first meeting between teacher and student, and surprisingly it often can create a writer or mold one already there but hungry, angry, or bewildered. In addition, a rewrite of the first paper, which is usually a result of the first interview, is a happy experience for both parties involved: it teaches the teacher that his job is rewarding and important; it teaches the student that he can do better; it shows both that they are involved in a creative, cooperative enterprise of which the papers are the fruit. Or will be.

The First Papers Generally

To return to the first papers, bad as they might be. The assignment was, of course, a description of a place, and the errors abound. The punctuation rules have scotched future errors of like kind; the individual lists of clichés will help. But what about the general errors and the papers in general?

For one thing, the papers will lack details. Outside of the clichés, they will speak of a lake without describing where it is, what it looks like, or how it smells and sounds on a July morning. They will speak of crowds in Grand Central Station without listing any of the types of people, faces, clothes, or attitudes to be found there. They will write of a Kansas farm without mentioning the smells from the fields, the flatness of the land, the proximity of the house to the outbuildings, the crops harvested, or the people involved. It may very well be a Kansas farm which the writer visited as a child, but it will be a cardboard creation without smell or taste, voices, wind or rain. It will be Grand Central with "crowds." It will be the lake without movement or season.

Yet, as the students read their "good" papers, the class will make comments revealing the above.

And here is a chance to talk about the importance of the writer reading his work aloud.

It is not a timesaver for the teacher. The teacher has read each paper (in this case, the first paper) already. He has graded, corrected, and commented upon it. But the writer has not yet been made aware that he has an audience and has been writing for an audience. For the ordinary, good-hearted citizen who wants to write—or, for that matter, the unordinary, bad-hearted citizen who wants to do the same thing—it is surprisingly valuable to read what he has written to an audience of his peers, to listen to their comments, and to answer their questions.

The reading of the first papers should take one class session or perhaps two. Within the semester's work, at least one

29

paper should be read aloud to the class by each student—better two, and best of all three. The results are manifold: the student discovers that he is writing for an audience; the class discovers that it is listening critically and is becoming more critical of its own writing; and the student ego is served.

VI

Session Five: People

The interviews have been given, at least for the complainers and the most bewildered, the punctuation rules have been memorized and tested, and the first papers have been read by the teacher, returned, and read aloud to the class by some of the students—all, one hopes, with good results.

Where are you? You are, of course, at the beginning of a writing class, and the students are generally interested. Nevertheless, how many models should be read to them for the second paper? And whose?

You might ask the class to write a second paper without using any aids other than the elements of good writing written on the blackboard, behind you and in front of them. And you might give suggestions.

The second paper should be a description of a person. The

teacher might begin by asking the class to discuss the most important ways by which a person unconsciously reveals himself. Is it by his walk? By his skeletal structure or the shape of his mouth (his most mobile feature), his eyes (the proverbial windows of the soul), his clothes, chosen carefully to reveal his self-image, however unconscious, his occupation, his mannerisms (twitching, ear-pulling, stammering), his neatness or lack of it, his personal evirons, office, room, apartment, house? By his relationships? By his goals or dreams, fears or obsessions?

When all these aspects of personality are discussed by the class, it is clear that they are too many. To make a clear portrait, the writer must choose only a few of the ways in which persons are revealed—unless he is writing a psychology textbook. And the writer must emphasize and dramatize these, and discount others.

If a person, for example, is ostensibly greedy, the fact that he has blond hair is not important; his greediness is. If he is poverty-stricken but blue-eyed, his poverty must be emphasized in all its tragedy. And if he is naïve beyond the point of general good will, like Candide, it doesn't matter that he is the possible inheritor of a farm in Nebraska. In other words, the outstanding qualities or features of a person must be those the writer chooses to emphasize. Yet there must be a reasonably wide range of them. In order for the portrait to have fullness and to convince, the qualities must be chosen from a group of general features in which we all share.

And these characteristics can be listed on the blackboard:

1. Personal environment
2. Occupation
3. Outstanding physical characteristics such as weight, age, sex, general attractiveness, or lack of it

4. Major relationships such as wife, husband, child, parent, employer
5. Chief hope or chief fear
6. Daily routine

There are many more as every actor knows who can reveal personality merely by a lisp, by plucking the lower lip, or by a single grimace. But the writers in your class must have a general list to begin with in order to make choices from them in relation to importance.

Here is an example of a student theme, a real one, which describes a person. It is a "D" paper. But then most of your early student papers will be.

A DEVIL OF AN ANGEL

Five feet eight inches and eighty pounds of devil. This is an average description for a baby of eleven, but my brother Mike stands out as an individual in all other ways. His soft, dark brown hair matches the chestnuts of the autumn trees. His dark brown eyes shimmer with the glee that little boys are capable of. Slim and soft are his virgin lips that manifest his constant child-like giggle. His walk and clothes reflect his thoughts and actions. When he is in his blue jeans and sweat shirt, his walk is sluggish, sloppy, and carefree. This is an indication of play-time where he reveals the personality traits inherited from his older brothers. Compatible to all (with the exception of the opposite sex) he holds his friends in high esteem. Hair combed in place and clothes of the latest styles, his walk is straight and full of confidence. In school he reveals the scholarship traits of his older brothers. Mike is also an altar boy in our church. Clothed in his cassock, we can hear his clear response to the priest and watch him execute his duties precisely. Being of Italian nationality, his temperament is touchy, but he cools down just as fast.

His experiences let him lead the life of a mischievous eleven-year-old. Getting into trouble is his chief trait, but his warm, considerate heart overcomes his devil-like mannerisms. His goals are varied from week to week, but they all indicate one main goal, to be someone of importance that will contribute to the good of the profession he chooses and to make my parents proud of their son.

As was said, this is a typical second paper from a typical college writing class. And its most glaring fault, its lack of clarity ("Clothed in his cassock, we . . . ," "baby boy," "Hair combed in place and clothes of the latest styles, his walk . . .") can be remedied by a second draft. The student, of course, will think the paper marvelous, and the teacher will have something of a bad time convincing him that it is not, showing him just where the elements of good writing have been forgotten, where the clichés are, and where generalization has been substituted for specific detail.

And because there *are* some elements of good writing in the paper, such as contrast (which the teacher will have commented upon praisefully), the student will be harder to convince than if he had used none at all.

The old journalistic rule of showing who-what-why-when-and-where might be a point of departure for teacher comments.

For example, we don't know the "devil's" family name or place of residence. Had the student written, "Michael Genovese, eleven years old, larkey, and his own boy, is growing up in Newark, New Jersey . . ." we would at least know where we are. And the clichés and generalizations can be marked by the teacher and will appear less often, probably, in paper three: "clothes of the latest styles," "lead a life," "brown eyes shimmer," "contribute to the good of the profession he chooses." These can be caught immediately and changed.

34

But essentially we need the child himself and not a generalized portrait of an American child. The writer in his second draft must show Mike in the midst of his schoolfellows and altar boys as someone different because of his own characteristics. We must hear him—dialogue may not be necessary in all characterizations but here it is useful—and see him much more clearly, in much more detail in order to understand him.

And all the sentences should not be of equal length.

But there will be some good papers in which the beginnings of really good writing will be seen by the class when the papers are read aloud. These papers can be saved by the students as kernels of their later short stories.

For the teacher who believes in models, here is a short one taken from the Nordhoff and Hall *Mutiny on the Bounty*—and cut and rewritten for class purposes:

To a modern eye the devil incarnate is Captain William Bligh. Aged twenty-nine at the time of the *Bounty*'s sailing, he was a merchant sailor turned warrior. Given to shouting his commands, he often lost his voice entirely and indicated his orders by frowns and rigid fingers. Although he was short, stout, and bandy-legged, his abilities as a navigator early in his career won for him a rating of master in the King's Navy.

At Copenhagen he commanded the *Gallton* to Lord Nelson's satisfaction, yet he lacked many of the qualities which one expects to find in an officer and a gentleman. He had no tact, his temper was vile, his stubborn will knew no compromise. In 1808 these qualities lost for him the governorship of New South Wales, as in 1789 they cost him his command aboard the *Bounty*. But in the end, despite his failings, he died a vice-admiral of the Blue.

Mr. Christian would no doubt add to the above, yet it remains a full portrait in few words. And it is not general.

And after the portraits, the good ones, have been read aloud by their authors, ask the students how the people described might behave in a crisis—a disaster at sea, for example, wartime bombing, the loss of a long-held and important job. You might ask the class if these persons could be clearly distinguished in a crowd or seen as being twenty years older, i.e., do we know enough about them to imagine them *as being* twenty years older?

Here is another illustration of characterization. Again, it is from Isak Dinesen and could be read to the students either before or after they do their own portraits. Each paper they write, after all, is simply an experiment and some time within the semester it might be well to tell the class as much, adding that their grades (although listed in your record book in order to fulfill the university's requirements) will be only an approximation.

Old Knudsen, the Dane, had come to the farm, sick and blind, and stayed there for the time it took him to die, a lonely animal. He walked along the roads all bent over his misery; for long periods he was without speech, for he had no strength left over from the hard task of carrying it, or, when he spoke, his voice, like the voice of the wolf or hyena, was in itself a wail.

But when he recovered breath, and for a little while was without pain, then sparks flew from the dying fire once more. He would then come to me and explain how he had got to fight with a morbid disposition in himself, an absurd tendency to see things black. It must be outreasoned, for the outward circumstances, they were not amiss, they were, the devil take him, not to be despised. Only pessimism, pessimism—that was a bad vice!

It was Knudsen who advised me to burn charcoal and sell it to the Indians of Nairobi, at a time when we were, on the farm, more than usually hard up. There were thousands of rupees in it, he assured me. And it could not fail under the aegis of Old Knudsen. . . .

I learned much about Knudsen's past life, and the strange adventures that had fallen to him wherever he had wandered. You had, in these conversations, to talk of Old Knudsen himself, the one righteous man,—or you would sink into that black pessimism against which he was warning you. He had experienced many things: shipwrecks, plague, fishes of unknown colouring, drinking-bouts, water-spouts, three contemporaneous suns in the sky, false friends, black villainy, short successes and showers of gold that instantly dried up again. . . . He was a born rebel, he saw a comrade in every outlaw. . . . He liked to talk of kings and royal families, jugglers, dwarfs and lunatics, for them he took to be outside the law. But for the good citizen he had a deep contempt, and law-abidingness in any man was to him the sign of a slavish mind. . . . He did not even respect, or believe in, the law of gravitation, which I learnt while we were felling trees together; he saw no reason why it should not be—by unprejudiced, enterprising people— changed into the exact reverse.

Hence Old Knudsen. And we see him, hear him, know him, and understand him, as the writer wished.

Because everyone is a student of human nature, there will be much comment upon these second papers, or those which you, as teacher, marked "Read," enough discussion perhaps for two or three class sessions. And one might tell the class at this point that a combination of setting and characterization, of place and person, needs only a motor action (a plot) and a theme to become a short story.

VII

Session Six (or Seven):
A Point of View

Early in your class meetings, and certainly in your personal interviews, you will find that each of your students "feels" that what he has to express in itself determines the success of his writing—that you, his teacher, are mentally retarded not to grasp at once what he is driving at. In other words, you will be bombarded by the theory that art (in this case, writing) is creative and any attempt to emphasize anything other than this fact is an indication of your own pedantry. It is not unusual to hear, audibly muttered by a student clutching an "F" paper: "Those who can, do; those who can't, teach."

It is prudent, therefore, to assign a "thought" paper for theme three. It will emphasize to even the most injured student that outline and form are necessities.

39

The outline will be different from any your students have used before. It will get them to think about emphasis and the relation of emphasis to self-expression, and it will give them all kinds of tricks to examine their logic or lack of logic.

You might begin by talking about the popularity of speech-making in American life. Mary O'Toole, Cynthia Seymour, Terese di Palma, and Maria Gomez, as the New York subway ads list them in an advertisement for soup, all may someday be called upon to make a speech. In planning their speeches they will be using a form. And the chief reason for this form is *emphasis.*

And emphasis, as you might tell your class, will not scotch self-expression but rather will make it possible. All points are not equal, all ideas do not deserve the same amount of space. A good outline—for a speech, an essay, or even the plot of a short story—should look something like an old-fashioned lady's corset. Above all, the main idea, the main point, should be *placed* so that the reader or listener is prepared for it. It should be about two-thirds of the way through the speech or essay. It should be a particular, rather than a general, idea or point. And it should answer a question.

The outline form, which you ought to draw clearly on the blackboard, noting that each band is of a different length, will look like the one on p. 41.

Suppose (you might say to the assembled students) your subject for an essay or speech were "The PTA and the Community," and your specific assignment a twenty-minute speech or a three-hundred-word article. How would you go about filling in this ridiculous-looking outline then?

"What about the Introduction and Conclusion?" one of the students might ask.

"Where are Roman numerals I and II?"

Well, the reason that Introduction, Conclusion and, as it's

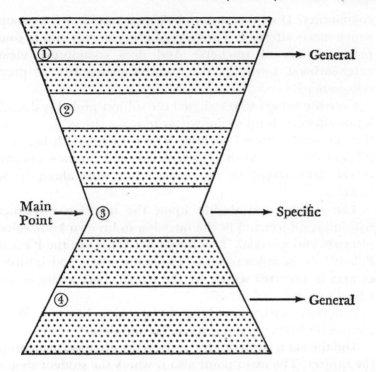

called, Body of the Paper, are not in the outline is that the words are meaningless and guide the writer nowhere. They do not create either emphasis or form. The word Introduction generally allows the student writer to produce a rambling page without a single idea; Conclusion might mean, and usually does, an unnecessary summary of what has been said before. Body of the Paper can, and does, mean anything.

One of the chief faults of student papers is that they have no main idea. Instead, they have a series of sometimes related ideas, all of equal importance and nearly all dealt with at equal length.

The first step is to shrink the subject. What PTA? What

community? Does this mean one's own specific PTA group, which meets alternate Tuesdays of every month and is comprised mainly of teachers? And does community mean neighborhood, township, the business community, or property owners?

Since the person who assigned the subject probably doesn't know either, it is up to the writer to make the subject fit the time or space allotted to him. The subject might be: The PTA of P.S. 104 and the Homeowners and Business Owners in the Area Served by the School. But what about it? So what?

The writer must decide upon the question contained within his subject and fit the question to his own knowledge, interests, and material. This might be: What can the PTA of P.S. 104 do in order to make the homeowners and business owners in the area served by the school more aware of the school's services and needs?

It doesn't matter how long the question becomes. What matters is whether or not it is specific and clear.

And the main point or idea answers the question made from the subject. The main point also is where the student should begin to make his outline, to fill in the spaces. The answer to the question, which is the main point, must be written out in sentence form, as all the other ideas must be written out as sentences within the outline form.

This will correct another recurring fault of student essays: the fact that the writer "gives away" his main idea at once and so has nothing to say of equal importance; or keeps his main point until the very end, drawing out suspense too long and leaving no time for a future "look" at his subject. In the first instance there is no suspense; in the second there is too much.

Therefore, the main point should be a detailed, particular

sentence answering the question into which the subject has been turned. And it should occur about two-thirds of the way through the essay or speech, because by then the reader or listener is ready for it.

Since the main point is the most important part of the essay, it should be decided upon first. The rest of the essay should be built around it.

The first point, upon which less time should be spent—hence the narrow band in the outline form—should be an idea which introduces the subject and thereby informs the listener about it. In relation to the PTA topic, it might be a good beginning to make the listener aware of the purpose of the PTA. The first point, or idea, might be: The PTA of P.S. 104 was established by a combined parent-teacher group in 1924 to make parents aware of what the teachers were teaching and to make teachers available to parents for any kind of consultation. Of course, the writer will develop this. He might describe what the neighborhood was like in 1924, what the school building looked like, where the first PTA meeting was held. But the essential first idea remains and should be written in the outline.

The second idea should be given more development and therefore more space. It might be the need for more neighborhood involvement because of the increasing importance of the PTA. The main point, which answers the question already made, the long question—What can the PTA of P.S. 104 do in order to make the homeowners and business owners in the area served by the school more aware of the school's services and needs?—has already been decided upon. It must be answered by a specific sentence, more specific than any other idea within the speech or essay. It might be a sentence (depending upon the writer's purpose) that reads

43

something like this: The PTA of P.S. 104 must undertake a campaign consisting of news releases to the local papers, pamphlets distributed to stores and offices within the area served by the school, and community social functions such as dances or card tournaments in order to elicit contributions and to extend information about the PTA's enlarged activities. (This sounds like a corker, but the sentences of an "idea" outline are not good writing and aren't meant to be; they must simply get everything "in.")

The last point might look to the future in order to indicate what can be accomplished, and has already been accomplished, when responsible members of a community have worked intimately with a PTA group.

Thus the outline is finished, a group of four detailed but simple sentences. Examples, statistics, case histories, elaborations all may be included in the paper or speech, but they do not belong in the outline. The ratio of two to one—that is, of two ideas leading to the main idea and one idea following the main idea—can be expanded as the length of time or amount of space is expanded. A forty-minute speech will contain twice as many ideas (though only one main idea) as a twenty-minute one, and a thousand-word essay may have as many as six ideas leading to the main idea and then two following.

But after the outline has been made it must be reviewed by the writer. If two ideas are the same, or nearly so, for example, the outline will show it and should be changed. If the first idea is specific rather than general, or if the main idea is not specific enough, the writer can correct his outline before he writes his paper.

Is this outline really usable—and used? There are myriad examples to show that it is, in both essays and speeches. Here is one of them:

Fourscore and seven years ago our fathers brought forth on this continent a new nation, conceived in liberty, and dedicated to the proposition that all men are created equal. Now we are engaged in a great civil war, testing whether that nation, or any nation so conceived and so dedicated, can long endure. We are met on a great battlefield of that war. We have come to dedicate a portion of that field as a final resting-place for those who here gave their lives that that nation might live. It is altogether fitting and proper that we should do this.

But in a larger sense we cannot dedicate, we cannot consecrate, we cannot hallow this ground. The brave men, living and dead, who struggled here have consecrated it, far above our poor power to add or detract. The world will little note, nor long remember what we say here, but it can never forget what they did here. It is for us, the living, rather, to be dedicated here to the unfinished work which they who fought here have thus far so nobly advanced. It is rather for us to be here dedicated to the great task remaining before us—that from these honored dead we take increased devotion to that cause for which they gave the last full measure of devotion—that we here highly resolve that these dead shall not have died in vain—that this nation, under God, shall have a new birth of freedom—and that government of the people, by the people, and for the people, shall not perish from the earth.

It is helpful of course if the teacher will read this well-known speech aloud in all its glory, asking the students to outline it as they listen. There will be, or should be, five points or ideas including the main point. The students then can read their outlines aloud or copy them on the blackboard. And it will be helpful for you, the teacher, to review the notable examples of The Elements of Good Writing which the speech-essay contains; the repetition of the letter sound *f* in the first sentence, the repetition of the word "here" throughout the essay (occurring eight times!), the arrangement of long and short sentences.

In relation to their own essays, it will be helpful if the students announce their subjects in class, for the first subjects chosen probably will be too broad for a two- or three-page paper. Together, teacher and class can "boil down" the subjects and change them into specific questions.

In any case, the essay's outline should be the next assignment. If the teacher prefers, the outline and the essay can be handed in at one time. But with most writing classes, the outline form, important as it is, is the Rubicon. After crossing it, or after several crossings, the importance of form and emphasis should have been learned.

VIII

The "Peanut Theme"; The Writer's Notebook; Pep Talks

We all can describe events: we drove down to the super-market and Mrs. Heinzelmann, the butcher's wife, announced her move to Dallas, Texas, already affecting a southern drawl. . . . On the way home we saw an accident and couldn't dispel the sight of the poor little spaniel in the middle of the road. . . . Mrs. Jones called again for the Community Chest drive and behaved rudely because *she* thought we'd contributed too little last year. . . .

Yet, as everyone knows, if two or more observers were to describe the same scene, the details, even the important ones, would be contradictory.

One of the ways to develop a "writer's eye" is of course to write, and write often. This means a notebook. (And more of this later.) A way to demonstrate to your students that they do *not* observe accurately, and should, is to give them a class writing assignment wherein they all describe a similar object and then read what they have written aloud to one another, and to you.

And an object easily procured, cheap, and unusual enough to interest the class as an *objet d'art,* an object anyway for art, is the peanut. In addition, it has plenty of sensory appeal; it can be seen in detail, it can be felt, heard, smelled, and tasted. And it resembles—animal, vegetable, or mineral? It connotes.

Buy a bag of peanuts in the shell and give one to each student. Let the students talk with one another as they write their papers (since they will anyway) , and this time it may be stimulating for them to exchange observations. And when the papers are read, first by those students who are the most eager, the others will question the accuracy of the detail; they will compare it with their own. As always, they will remember the elements of good writing and criticize a monotonous sentence structure, lack of contrast, too much visual description, and so on.

If there should be time during the class session, the "peanut" paper will lead into a discussion of the writer's notebook, which ought to be given as a long-range assignment, perhaps with dated entries. (This will mean that you can read the notebooks at the end of the semester and be reasonably certain that the student hasn't written the entire assignment in one evening—which would do him no good at all.)

The Writer's Notebook

The notebook can contain almost whatever the student chooses to write. There should be some minimum requirements which can be listed, either mimeographed beforehand or dictated during a class period. There should be several descriptions of places, one or two brief characterizations, bits of dialogue heard and noted, perhaps on a subway or a bus. And there should be essay outlines and plot outlines, exercises like the "peanut theme"—a paper perhaps on a glass of water or a single tree—and notes for the first chapter of a novel. The notebook should be filled at the end of the semester, and that is its chief purpose.

Pep Talks

If confidence were an integral part of human nature the whole history of the human family would be different. Confidence isn't, of course, and a major chore of any teacher of any art is to instill it in his students, at least to try to. With students of writing this is partially accomplished by having each student read his best work aloud, call for comments, and reply to class comments. It is partially accomplished by the affirmative criticism, the "messages" which each corrected paper must contain—advice from the teacher but also praise. Even such old acorns as "I know you can do better," "This shows promise," "A good job," "Bravo!" "This rings the bell!" are fuel for the creative sparks and enthusiasm without which any writing dies aborning. Pep talks are never irrelevant. Some classes, and some students, need more rather then fewer of them. The teacher knows best, just as the teacher always knows best about his or her class—this book is merely suggestions.

If, for example, the class criticism of a student paper is entirely negative, the teacher should intrude. He might say to the class, "Don't you think, though, that Mr. Jones does have some effective physical description here?" In spite of the fact that Mr. Jones may have forgotten dialogue, setting, contrast, variety in sentence structure, as has been pointed out, he *did* have good physical description and the class should say so.

If a student's papers do not improve, a friendly and encouraging interview with the student is in order—and may work. Sometimes the discouraged teacher must give himself a pep talk during the semester. Good writing, after all, takes time for you to teach and for the students to learn. Suddenly, sometimes even the worst student "catches on."

Examples of successful authorship, after unpromising beginnings, abound and can be read to the class. One of the most interesting examples is the first draft of Keats' "Ode to a Grecian Urn." This, read to the class and followed by a reading of the finished poem, is invaluable therapy. Passages from Hemingway's first novel, *Torrents of Spring* (Hemingway again because the class will have read at least one of his stories or novels), can be read for their awkwardness, their bad writing. For the same reasons William Faulkner's first novel, *Mosquitoes,* is useful followed by the best passages from *The Sound and the Fury* perhaps or *Light in August.* The moral of these illustrations, which is the importance of effort, needs no illustration at all.

Here are two drafts of a passage by T. E. Lawrence from his monumental *Seven Pillars of Wisdom.* The second and final version was written during a period of seven years and represents much reworking:

> The dead lay naked under the moon. Turks are much whiter-skinned than the Arabs among whom I had been living, and these were mere boys. Close around them lapped the dark wormwood, now heavy with dew and sparkling like sea-spray. Wearied in mind and body, I felt that I would rather be of this quiet company than with the shouting, restless mob farther up

the valley, boasting of their speed and strength, and quarreling over the plunder. For however this campaign might go with its unforeseen toils and pains, death must be the last chapter in the history of every man of us.

Compare:

The dead men looked wonderfully beautiful. The night was shining gently down, softening them into new ivory. Turks were white-skinned on their clothed parts, much whiter than the Arabs; and these soldiers had been very young. Close around them lapped the dark wormwood, now heavy with dew, in which the ends of the moonbeams sparkled like sea-spray. The corpses seemed flung so pitifully on the ground, huddled anyhow in low heaps. Surely if straightened they would be comfortable at last. So I put them all in order, one by one, very wearied myself, and longing to be of these quiet ones, not of the restless, noisy, aching mob up the valley, quarreling over the plunder, boasting of their speed and strength to endure God knew how many toils and pains of this sort, with death, whether we won or lost, waiting to end the history.

The clichés, the "mere boys" and "every man of us," have gone. The monotonously even sentences have been re-arranged. The contrast has been heightened by the inclusion of more detail, more adjectives, and by Lawrence's own activity in moving the dead (whether or not he actually did so is beside the point). And verbs like "flung" and "huddled" have been substituted for a passive verb like "lay." The wormwood is not now sparkling "like sea-spray," but it is the "ends of the moonbeams" that sparkle, adding at the same time detail and symbol. For the moon is a dead planet and its light is cold.

The teacher can rewrite his own favorite passages upon

occasion. It is pleasant entertainment and a surprise to the class when they hear the original and see for themselves how good writing becomes bad by scratching out its "elements." For example:

The reader could possibly assume that my name is Ishmael, the son of Abraham and Hagar, who was exiled as a wanderer in days gone by, for in recent years I undertook a whaling trip in order to buttress my financial position. Since I hoped that this voyage would alter my equally depressed state of mind, I prescribed an ocean voyage for myself, basing my conclusions on the fact that most human beings are drawn to the ocean as a panacea for the human condition.

Of course it is Melville, and this is what he really wrote in *Moby Dick:*

Call me Ishmael. Some years ago—never mind how long precisely—having little or no money in my purse, and nothing particular to interest me on shore, I thought I would sail about a little and see the watery part of the world. It is a way I have of driving off the spleen and regulating the circulation. Whenever I find myself growing grim about the mouth; whenever it is a damp, drizzly November in my soul; whenever I find myself involuntarily pausing before coffin warehouses, and bringing up the rear of every funeral I meet; and especially whenever my hypos get such an upper hand of me that it requires a strong moral principle to prevent me from deliberately stepping into the street and methodically knocking people's hats off—then, I account it high time to get to the sea as soon as I can. This is my substitute for pistol and ball. With a philosophical flourish Cato throws himself upon his sword; I quietly take to the ship. There is nothing surprising in this. If they but knew it, almost all men in their degree, some time or other, cherish very nearly the same feelings toward the ocean with me.

This kind of exercise is itself a pep talk. The students will discover that good writing is not magically achieved, that it is achieved by means of the same elements they themselves are working with. And they will hear great prose.

IX

The Research Paper

Most universities require that a research paper be written in the first-year writing course. It is an important assignment within the course, perhaps the most important. The student's future success in other courses depends upon learning the techniques of research and research writing. Indeed, in most college classes the research or term paper represents one-third of the grade. But even in a writing class aimed at expression-plus-organization-plus-form, the research paper is important. People who are not college students also write reports—engineers do, lawyers do, home economists do, PTA members do—and it would be culling from your course an important form of writing, one closer perhaps to the needs of your students than the short story or the novel, to omit the research paper from your assignments.

It is good sense for the teacher to assume that no student in the class has done research before. It is also good sense to assign the paper well before the end of the semester, and to require that it be handed in piecemeal: bibliography, research cards, outline, and text.

But it is also important that the student write on a subject meaningful to him.

And this means an interview.

For each student may not know really what he is interested in. And if he does have a major interest, such as the American Civil War, he may need prodding in order to shrink his subject to malleable size.

Example:

Teacher: You say you don't know what to write about. Yet you've been working in the steelmills here for a long time, fifteen years as you've said. Doesn't anything about the work interest you?

Student: The paycheck.

Teacher: Is it adequate? I mean for your family's needs?

Student: It's all right.

Teacher: Have you had any raises recently?

Student: The union got us a raise in sixty-two.

Teacher: What union?

Student: Our local. We threatened a walkout and they gave in. They didn't want no trouble and knew we'd give it to 'em like we did in fifty-eight.

Teacher: What happened in fifty-eight?

Student: We shut down. Some of us stayed in the plant three, four weeks. The local sent in food, plenty of cigarettes. We didn't have it so bad.

Teacher: That's a wonderful subject for a short story. You know the scene and you've got a dramatic conflict right off the bat. The suspense is built up in terms of how long the men can hold out. But I don't think it's right for a research paper. How about doing a paper on the establishment of unions in this country? You know, Samuel Gompers and the Wobblies and some of the early strikes. For one thing, I'd like to know more about the subject.

Student: Couldn't get no books.

Teacher: What do you mean you couldn't get books? There must be all kinds of books on unions in the public library.

Student: No. I looked.

Teacher: How do you mean you looked when you haven't planned to do a research paper before?

Student: I was there looking up books on premature babies, so I got interested and looked around.

Teacher: What books about babies?

Student: My wife didn't know what was wrong and we had our first come early, six months. For a couple of weeks it looked like she wouldn't be normal. I mean the baby. She didn't see right, move, or anything.

Teacher: Is she all right now?

Student: She's fine, thank God. The doctor told me a lot of premature babies are like that.

Teacher: But you didn't know that then?

Student: Know what?

Teacher: What the symptoms were—I mean the normal symptoms after a premature birth. Maybe that's your question.

Student: You mean for this research paper?

Teacher: Why not?

Note: The above is not an attempt to make fun of bad grammar—nor of students. It is an attempt to indicate how many American students, both college-age and adult, do speak. If the teacher finds this distasteful, he must either get

57

used to it or else change his profession. And if he feels that grammar is an indication of intelligence or of writing ability, he must change his job and become a teacher of grammar or speech. The cause for good grammar in America has been lost for years. And it has been my experience, anyway, that a student of writing will teach himself grammar, once he is really writing, because he will fall in love with words and the language. As a matter of fact, the steelworker, who was a real student of mine some years ago, did write a fine research paper on premature births and went on to write another on Lincoln's early years as a lawyer since, as it turned out, he was interested in law and also in Lincoln.

Usually, the student will want to be told what to write about. The point is that it is far better for him to decide.

Example:

Student: You say we have to write about something we're interested in. Well, what I'm interested in you wouldn't even look at. I'd get a "F" before I start.

Teacher: Why?

Student: Because you don't want real writing, Henry Miller, Ferlinghetti, Corso. You want stuff about guys that've been dead a hundred years. Melville! Who reads Melville any more? And Lawrence was a queer. Everybody knows that.

Teacher: He wasn't a queer. All his biographers make that perfectly clear.

Student: Well, who cares about somebody that wrote a hundred years ago? These guys you think are good weren't even with it. Hemingway was no tough guy.

Teacher: Like Miller?

Student: Yeah, like Miller. He's honest. He's with it. You read one page of Miller and you get told something. Those other guys write with their feet. You take one page of *Tropic*——

58

Teacher: *Tropic of Cancer?*

Student: *Tropic of Cancer, Capricorn,* what's the difference? Anyway, one page is like a spotlight. I mean it.

Teacher: Well, why not write about Henry Miller, what he contributed to American fiction, what his influences were, whom he influenced, and so on? Your question might be, What is the importance of Henry Miller's work to modern American fiction?

Student: He's not dead.

Teacher: Nobody said you had to write about someone dead.

Student: I thought we did.

Thus the interview, and the research question, the answer to which is, of course—the main point and the central idea of the old-fashioned corset outline—to be used in the research paper.

It is useful to keep a record of the question each student has chosen to answer in his paper. This will prevent his changing the question later on if he finds insufficient books and periodicals on his subject. It will prevent his choosing a subject inappropriate for a research paper, one that can be answered by a single word. (An unpleasantly popular topic in recent years is: Does Smoking Cause Lung Cancer? Which can be answered, without research, by saying, "It might.")

Research Cards

Or Mother's recipe cards, which can be bought in any dimestore, provide a red-lined upper margin for categories and blue lines for quick, readable notes, and come in large, middle, and small sizes, although the middle-sized are the best.

It is necessary to draw a research card with large lines on the blackboard. In the upper right-hand corner of the card goes the name of the book and the pages which the notes on the card refer to. Above the red line goes the category—actually, a condensed statement of the point or idea into which the card falls with its information. In an eight- to ten-page research paper, there should be about twelve ideas, including the main idea, which is the answer to the question made on the subject, just as in the earlier short essay. On the card's blue lines the student will write his notes, using information from his sources but condensing it, setting it down in his own words. There should be, roughly, for a research paper of ten pages, about fifty cards. Some of the students will hand in a hundred cards and others will hand in only twenty. But fifty is the goal. Also, many of the cards will be "repeats," that is, they will contain the same information as the student has found and recorded from earlier books, and therefore will not be usable. Also, the student should write on only one side of the card, in order to save the trouble of turning them over. And here—in an ordinary college class rather than in an adult, evening class—the teacher can remind his students that they will be writing three or four research papers per semester in their college years, and that any time-saving tricks are valuable.

Because of their importance, the research cards should be carefully read and graded by the teacher. The student should arrange them by categories or "ideas" in relation to the order of the ideas in his outline—that is, the group of cards related to the first idea should come first. The cards should not be numbered, for the categories or ideas may be rearranged.

It is helpful, time permitting, for the teacher to talk with each student about his research cards. Does the student see, for example, the necessity of noting on each card the pages of the source it refers to? Does he understand that a research paper is a rearrangement, a rewording of material he has found, and not merely a copied version of it? Does he understand how the cards are to be used in writing the essay?

Two weeks should be time enough for your students to prepare their research cards. There are other parts to the paper, such as the footnote and bibliography pages, which will require emphasis and time. Yet the teacher must make certain that the research cards are satisfactory as they are, of course, the raw material of the text itself. Fifty adequate research cards will not produce a good paper, but they will go a long way in assuring its success.

Bibliography

("I can't find the books." "I can't find five books." "I tried to use *The New York Times Index,* but our librarian never heard of it." "I can't find two periodicals on ancient Egyptian burial customs. They weren't writing periodicals then." "My brother goes to Northwestern and he has a writing teacher that didn't make them do a research paper at all." "What good is it?")

A sensible assignment for the bibliography is a minimum of five books and two periodicals. This will prevent too much dependence on one or two books and will also give some experience in periodical research. *The New York Times Index* is, of course, invaluable, but it is not always available in small libraries. Nevertheless, the number of periodicals pertaining to special fields—medicine, art history, literature (ancient and modern), military history—staggers the mind. The student *can* find two periodicals and five books; if his subject is so esoteric or his question so specific that he cannot find them, interview him again and change both.

The bibliography, properly done with author's last name first, should come in to the teacher about a week after the first research-paper interview.

Footnotes

In order to emphasize the truth that the research paper does not represent original thought by the student but only original arrangement of other people's ideas, the teacher should insist on a minimum of one footnote per paragraph. And he should emphasize the fact that the research paper has no room at all for the writer's opinions; his opinions will determine the arrangement of his categories only—and, of course, the question he has made out of his subject. Since the papers should be typed, insist that the footnote numbers, in parentheses, be placed one space above the final sentence of each source. (A paragraph taken from one source will have one footnote above its last sentence; a paragraph from two sources will have two footnotes, etc.) A direct quotation, of course, must be footnoted immediately no matter where it occurs within the paragraph.

There are two fashions of footnoting. One is to list all footnotes at the bottom of each page, a major problem for the writer-typist. Another, and equally respectable, is to list all footnotes on a footnote page at the end of the text. The footnotes in this case will be listed consecutively, and ditto marks can be used.

General Comments on the Research Paper

Since the majority of your students will not have written a research paper before, be fussy. Announce to the class that the purpose of life, after all, may be simply the pursuit of excellence and that excellence is the goal of the research-paper assignment. This may be news to some of them but to all it will be a spur. In regard to the paper, ask for a cardboard cover (price five cents), a paper free from spelling or punctuation errors (you might refuse to read those pages with more than one spelling error), and a title page with title of paper, name of author, place of writing (your school and your city), and the date submitted clearly stated, and with the title and author stated again at the head of page one.

It is wise to assign the paper itself for a time close to, but not at the end of, the semester. You must read, mark, grade, and return them, and some may have to be rewritten. One or two might be publishable; you will have to ferret out small publications or, at the least, see the paper through publication in the college or university literary magazine. And this takes time.

A Speech

Since many universities require that their teacher of writing be also a teacher of speech, the put-upon teacher of writing has a natural spring for speeches in the research cards. With them, the student has notes upon a subject in which he is, temporarily, an enthusiast and an authority. He may need graphs or maps as illustrations, and these are available. Although a good writer is not necessarily a good speaker, a student writer will not be hampered by giving a speech from his research cards. It might, indeed, improve his final research paper, or stimulate him to do further research if areas of his talk, and subject, should seem unclear to his audience.

The speech, if necessary, can be preceded by a class session given to the elements of speech-making, and during the speeches the class can take notes for comments upon the subject matter and the presentation. At the least, a speech from research cards will clarify a student's thinking before he begins to write his paper; it will reveal to him, importantly, how little his audience knows about his pet subject and how carefully and cautiously he must expound upon it.

X

Narration

Or plot. What is a plot? It is a series of incidents with a beginning, a middle, and an end. Like theme, characterization, and setting, it is one of the four elements of fiction (which will be talked about later when the students are ready to write a short story), and it is perhaps the most important of these four elements. Plot is what happens. Alone, it is the tale told by the idiot who cannot see the point of the story, who is unaware of the background (setting), and to whom all its characters or personages are of equal importance, and without past or future.

Plot contains conflict, suspense, resolution (or plot climax as distinguished from thematic climax), and the events are seldom told in exact chronological sequence; most plots, whether in stories, novels, or dramas, begin in the middle, go back to the beginning, and jump to the end.

All this can be described to the students before their next writing assignment, which is to tell a tale. It ought to be made clear to them that they are not to write a short story, that the assignment is simply to relate events, and that the result will be only one of the elements of fiction—a fragment of a story. The short story will come later.

It's not easy simply to tell a tale. The student might begin by writing "Once upon a time," a perfectly good beginning in itself, and a way to avoid elaborate characterization or description of place. The teacher might read a fairy tale to the class, for writers like the Brothers Grimm and Hans Christian Andersen, brief in their narration, are also brief in their descriptions of people and setting. "The Little Match Girl," "Cinderella," and "Rumpelstiltskin" are mostly plot—simple tales that will show the students what plot is.

Another illustration that will take somewhat longer to read might be any one of the short stories of Conan Doyle's *Memoirs of Sherlock Holmes.* Take away the delightful Holmes, and you have tales of pure plot. The story is introduced as soon as Holmes is hired, and the beginnings, told in flashbacks, mesh into the conflict and so to the discovery, or resolution.

Another illustration easily found in any collection of modern American short stories is Truman Capote's "Miriam." Briefly, a widow living alone in a New York City apartment, and unaware of her loneliness, meets a child outside a movie theater on a snowy Sunday evening. The child announces that her name is Miriam and asks to be taken into the theater. The woman, although struck by the fact that the girl is alone and is no more than ten or twelve, buys her a ticket. But once they are outside the theater again, the child disappears.

However, on a later evening, the child appears at the

woman's apartment and asks to be fed jam sandwiches and milk, complaining that there are no sugared almonds to eat. She examines the woman's jewelry and the neatness of the apartment—she says she will come back again. The woman meanwhile is frightened. She had not given her name or address to the child. How did the child find her? And upon ensuing afternoons, the widow is followed upon her solitary walks by a strange old man who seems to have some knowledge of Miriam; he does not speak but she senses that he knows of the visit. But the woman, in spite of herself, buys some sugared almonds.

Finally, Miriam comes again to the woman's apartment, bringing a cardboard box containing a doll and clothes. She says that she has come to stay. The woman runs in a panic to a neighbor's apartment and asks the startled couple to go to her apartment; she says that there is a little girl there who will not leave. Going upstairs and returning, the neighbor announces that there is no one in the woman's apartment; both he and his wife look at the widow, certain that she is insane. The widow returns to her apartment and finds it empty. She settles into her comfortable chair and into her loneliness, to compose herself. After a moment, she hears a voice from the bedroom and realizes that it is Miriam and that Miriam is talking to her.

The thematic implications of this story should not be stressed now but only the sequence of its events, the plot itself. Do any of the students have a friend or relative who was involved in an equally strange relationship, which *might* have been hallucination? The charming play *Harvey* is such an example. If there is no response to this question, you might ask the class whether they have known anyone involved in some sudden and dramatic event which unexpectedly changed a life—winning the Irish sweepstakes, perhaps, or first prize on a bonanza television show, or finding a long-lost parent or sibling? Usually, one or more of the students will produce an illustration. And as it is told to the class, you might suggest changes, the condensation of certain scenes perhaps, or the elimination of minor characters, or a different point of departure—perhaps the narration should begin closer to the discovery or plot climax.

This is a good time, too, to talk about narrative focus (that pedantically awkward name for the storyteller himself) since the students will have to decide before they begin to write just who is to tell their tale. Should it be told, for example, by the chief character? Is it perhaps better told by an author who knows everyone involved? Or should the narrator be someone who only heard the tale second- or third-hand?

The class can discuss this, relating the problem of narrative focus to the experiences they have just talked about. They will discover for themselves that certain tales are best told through one kind of narrator, others through another. A tale of hallucination or the supernatural, for instance, could hardly be told by the main character as successfully as by a minor one. Emily Brontë's great novel *Wuthering Heights* often mistakenly criticized for its insistence on minor characters as narrators, is effective partly because of its focus; because practical, not-too-imaginative visitors to the Heights have seen ghosts, we believe in those ghosts. Also, except in a Japanese movie, the dead cannot speak for themselves. If Miriam had told the Capote tale, we would know what she was up to, supernatural figure or not, and there would be no suspense and no mystery.

Other methods of narrative focus, letters, for example—and the famous World War II story, "Address Unknown," is worth looking up and reading aloud to the class—are equally good if they fit the plot. Even Faulkner's technique of naming a set of narrators who describe the same scene, almost like a set of dramatis personae, is effective when the purpose of the tale is to show "individual differences."

The possibilities of the assignment, in any case, should be dramatized by the teacher just as the fact that a tale is *not* a short story should be emphasized. Then the student himself must create, condense, and experiment with a tale.

XI

Recapitulation

Since your students are by now busily at work preparing their research cards in various libraries, and since you have given them quite as much information as the general student can or will take for the moment, it may be useful to repeat an assignment here. Since they will be struggling soon enough with their research-paper outlines and since they have just finished a narration, a possible reassignment should be either another characterization or a description of place. Either will show them, and you, what they have learned.

The following selection from Budd Schulberg's novel *The Harder They Fall* is useful in many ways. It appeals to the reader's five senses, for one thing. Its details are specifically and accurately seen. It includes dialogue which adds to the scene without introducing character. And it is fraught with contrast.

71

As you read the selection, or have the students read it, ask them to list the elements of good writing which it contains.

Americans are still an independent and rebellious people—at least in their reactions to signs. Stillman's gym, up the street from the Garden, offers no exception to our national habit of shrugging off prohibitions. Hung prominently on the gray, nondescript walls facing the two training rings, a poster reads: "No rubbish or spitting on the floor under penalty of the law." If you want to see how the boys handle this one, stick around until everybody has left the joint and see what's left for the janitor to do. The floor is strewn with cigarettes smoked down to their stained ends, cigar butts chewed to soggy pulp, dried spittle, empty match cases, thumbed and trampled copies of the *News, Mirror,* and *Journal,* open to the latest crime of passion or the race results, wadded gum, stubs of last night's fight at St. Nick's (managers comps), a torn-off cover of an Eighth Avenue restaurant menu with the name of a new matchmaker in Cleveland scrawled next to a girl's phone number. Here on the dirty gray floor of Stillman's is the telltale debris of a world as sufficient unto itself as a walled city of the Middle Ages.

You enter this walled city by means of a dark, grimy stairway that carries you straight up off Eighth Avenue into a large, stuffy, smoke-filled, hopeful, cynical, glistening-bodied world. The smells of this world are sour and pungent, a stale, gamey odor blended of sweat and liniment, worn fight gear, cheap cigars and too many bodies, clothed and unclothed, packed into a room with no noticeable means of ventilation. The sounds of this world are multiple and varied, but the longer you listen, the more definitely they work themselves into a pattern, a rhythm that begins to play in your head like a musical score: the tap-dance tempo of the rope-skippers; the three-minute bell; the footwork of the boys working in the ring, slow, open-gloved, taking it easy; the muffled sound of the flat, high-laced shoes on the canvas as the big name in next week's show at the Garden takes a sign from his manager and goes to work, crowding his sparring partner into a corner and shaking him up with body punches; the hard-breathing of the boxers, the rush of air through the fighter's fractured nose, in a staccato timed to his movements; the confidential tones the managers use on the matchmakers from the smaller clubs spotting new talent, *Irving, let me assure you, my boy loves to fight. He wants none of them easy ones. Sure he looked lousy Thursday night. It's a question of styles. You know that Ferrara's style was all wrong for him. Put 'em in with a boy who likes to mix it an' see the difference;* the deals, the arguments, the angles, the apprisals, the muted Greek chorus, muttering out of the corner of its mouth with a nervous cigar between its teeth; the noise from the telephones; the booths "For Outgoing Calls Only," *Listen, Joe, I just been talking to Sam and he says okay for two hundred for the semifinal at* . . . the endless ringing of the "Incoming Calls Only"; a guy in dirty slacks and a cheap yellow sports-shirt, cupping his hairy hands together and lifting his voice above the incessant sounds of the place: *Whitey Bimstein, call for Whitey Bimstein, anybody seen Whitey* . . .; the garbage-disposal voice of Stillman himself, a big, authoritative, angry-looking man, growling out the names of the next pair of fighters to enter the ring, loudly but always unrecognizably, like a fierce, adult babytalk; then the bell again, the footwork sounds, the thudding of gloves against hard bodies, the routine fury.

The atmosphere of this world is intense, determined, dedicated. The place swarms with athletes, young men with hard, lithe, quick bodies under white, yellow, brown, and blackish skins and serious, concentrated faces, for this is serious business, not just for blood, but for money.

All kinds of things could be done with the above, besides listing the elements of good writing. One exercise might be the substitution of inactive verbs and general adjectives for the active verbs and marvelously specific adjectives Schulberg has used. Another might be a rewrite of the passage using the same kind of dialogue it already contains but making dialogue the exclusive device for showing setting. And another might be an outline for a paper on your schoolroom with the same organization of sensory images as Schulberg's—that is, the general appearance of the room as seen from the corridor, significant debris such as posters, fire-drill directions, cigarette butts (possibly) , and the room itself with its sounds and inhabitants (teacher and pupils) , all creating the atmosphere and the tone.

Another characterization will give you an opportunity to repeat and emphasize its techniques. And since the student has already written one characterization, and corrected it, his experience in describing environment, occupation, physical description, relationships, hopes, goals, fears, and daily routine is close enough to add to and to learn other techniques. For this second character, for example, he might experiment with names. Someone named Heathcliff is not likely to work in a United States post office; Jane Eyre describes a plain girl—and if the student objects that a rose called a bougainvillea would smell as sweet, remind him of Mr. Micawber, Scarlett O'Hara, Uriah Heep, Babbitt, and others of the famous names in literature whose very sounds are characterization.

Other techniques would be a personal gesture or physical idiosyncrasy. Someone, for example, who is continually fiddling with his wedding ring (at least a well-fitted ring) , is most certainly thinking about another marriage or an end to his present one. Someone who walks stiffly erect is quite different in personality from his colleague who walks with a shambling slouch. A woman of fifty who is continually removing her eye glasses and putting them on again reveals to any observer that she doesn't like wearing them, wishes she didn't have to, wishes she were younger.

Again, clothes reveal character and can sometimes even

serve as symbols of it. Raskolnikov's ragged costume as he emerges from his room at the beginning of *Crime and Punishment* is less important in revealing Raskolnikov than the high top hat he also wears, ragged as that is too, but bizarrely askew, tilted, and fallen in, like his philosophy of the superman. The Man in the Brooks Brothers Suit reveals, by his very anonymity, what he is, whether he wants to be what he is or not. And the beatnik conformist, whose long hair, boots, loose, usually dirty shirt, and too-tight denim trousers are exactly like those of his friends, is telling anyone who cares about the unoriginality of his character and his ideas.

This time ask the students also to use characteristic speech in their portraits. Probably no writer but Dickens could imagine such revealing utterance as, "I shall never desert Mr. Macawber," or, "I'm a very 'umble man, Mr. Copperfield," or the immortal, "Barkis is willin'." But we can try.

And ask the students to use contrast also. It is possible in their second characterizations that they might want to describe two characters at one time, and this, too, is a technique of characterization. A dull postal clerk may have a brother who is a regular roustabout; to describe them both, perhaps at a family dinner where each behaves differently in the same situation, brings out the characters of both, makes both portraits brighter. The mild, virtuous Melanie in *Gone with the Wind* heightens the fierceness of Scarlett O'Hara, just as the callous selfishness of Mildred reveals the sensitivity and decency of Philip, the hero of Maugham's *Of Human Bondage*.

The students might even try a paragraph or two of stream of consciousness, and you might read them certain passages from Joyce's *Ulysses* to show what can be done with this.

By midterm, the dropouts will have disappeared; you are left with the interested students only. They will not object if this second characterization is aimed at as many as ten pages. By now, with few exceptions, they will want to write.

XII

The Short Story

So much has been written, so many "how to" books, on the short story that adding to them, even with one chapter, seems presumptuous. Yet the point is that too much *has* been said about the short story; it has been elaborated upon to such an extent that everyone is confused. There is no single formula for the short story; there are only elements. But these elements, the elements of fiction, have already been "done" by your students: they have written a setting, a characterization, an essay of ideas, and a tale. (The fifth element, style, cannot be taught. It will come as the students write and develop as writers, and this is about all the advice one can give about it.) What remains is for your students to put these elements into a form called the short story. And for you to describe this form before they write.

In essence, the short story is the discovery made by the main character of some eternal feature of the world and life. (This is true also of the novel, but the novel usually contains several main characters and several eternal features.) And this discovery usually creates some major change of attitude on the part of the discoverer.

Perhaps the best illustration of this definition is the so-called story of initiation. In it a boy or girl discovers some facet of the adult world and rises to meet it—whether or not the facet is an affirmative one. Sherwood Anderson's "I Want to Know Why," all of Hemingway's Nick Adams stories, and most of the fiction written particularly for teenagers, follow this pattern closely. The difference between this fiction and fiction written primarily for adults—the "great" stories of de Maupassant, Chekhov, and Conrad, of Pirandello and Mansfield and Dostoevski—is that the main character's discovery is usually one that condemns him, one that reveals his human vulnerability, his tragic human flaws.

And some fiction called "short story" is not that at all, but parable—Tolstoy's religious stories, for example. And some fiction called short story is really characterization, like many of the short sketches by Mark Twain.

But the definition holds generally, as the teacher will discover for himself when he examines his favorites in the genre. It is why the student writer, in attempting his first short story, should begin with theme. If the short story "turns upon" the main character's discovery, then that which he discovers about the world or himself *is* the theme.

The next step for the writer is to decide what kind of main character in what kind of setting would make such a discovery. And then what kind of force, what circumstance would propel him to it.

And in this way the short story is planned.

There are a few additional requirements: the short story must open very close to the discovery, and the flashbacks must be brief. In effect, the plot will go: near end, beginning, middle, and end. And this means, of course, that the main character must be shown at once, whereas in a novel he can be talked about for two or three chapters. The first paragraph or two of the short story must tell us the significant features of the main character as well as those of his environment (the setting) , and we must have almost at once some feeling of the conflict which will lead to his discovery and change.

There are many ways to achieve this arrangement of fictional elements. For students who are not accomplished short-story writers, however, the above will do.

From among the hundreds of short stories which are valuable for reading aloud to the class, I have found that Chekhov's "The Lament" (also known as "Misery") is the clearest and best. Therefore, although it is easy to obtain (it is included in the Modern Library collection of Chekhov stories, as well as in the helpful *Understanding Fiction* by Cleanth Brooks and Robert Penn Warren) , I have included it here. The teacher can simplify the Russian names as he reads, or substitute American ones, and there will be time in one class session to read the story twice. The question for the class to answer—How does "The Lament" reveal short-story form?—ought to occupy one or even two class sessions. The steps of the plot which bring the old cabdriver closer and closer to the discovery that no one will hear his lament, that no one will help him to bear his grief, correspond with the changes of his passengers and his frustrated conversation in the cab station. The first paragraph, in its almost perfect delineation of character—the bent, immobile man, and the small, bewildered horse—as well as the tone created by the description of setting—twilight and falling snow—deserve to be very carefully examined. Above all, the students should point out the moment of discovery.

THE LAMENT

It is twilight. A thick wet snow is twirling around the newly lighted street lamps, and lying in soft thin layers on roofs, on horses' backs, on people's shoulders and hats. The cabdriver Iona Potapov is quite white, and looks like a phantom; he is bent double as far as a human body can bend double; he is seated on his box; he never makes a move. If a whole snowdrift fell on him, it seems as if he would not find it necessary to shake it off. His little horse is also quite white, and remains motionless; its immobility, its angularity, and its straight wooden-looking legs, even close by, give it the appearance of a ginger-bread horse worth a *kopek*. It is, no doubt, plunged in deep thought. If you were snatched from the plow, from your usual gray surroundings, and were thrown into this slough full of monstrous lights, unceasing noise, and hurrying people, you too would find it difficult not to think.

Iona and his little horse have not moved from their place for a long while. They left their yard before dinner, and up to now, not a fare. The evening mist is descending over the town, the white lights of the lamps replacing brighter rays, and the hub-bub of the street getting louder. "Cabby for Viborg way!" suddenly hears Iona. "Cabby!"

Iona jumps, and through his snow-covered eyelashes sees an officer in a greatcoat, with his hood over his head.

"Viborg way!" the officer repeats. "Are you asleep, eh? Viborg way!"

With a nod of assent Iona picks up the reins, in consequence of which layers of snow slip off the horse's back and neck. The officer seats himself in the sleigh, the cabdriver smacks his lips to encourage his horse, stretches out his neck like a swan, sits up, and, more from habit than necessity, brandishes his whip.

The little horse also stretches its neck, bends its wooden-looking legs, and makes a move undecidedly.

"What are you doing, werewolf!" is the exclamation Iona hears from the dark mass moving to and fro, as soon as they have started.

"Where the devil are you going? To the r-r-right!"

"You do not know how to drive. Keep to the right!" calls the officer angrily.

A coachman from a private carriage swears at him; a passerby, who has run across the road and rubbed his shoulder against the horse's nose, looks at him furiously as he sweeps the snow from his sleeve. Iona shifts about on his seat is if he were on needles, moves his elbows as if he were trying to keep his equilibrium, and gapes about like someone suffocating, who does not understand why and wherefore he is there.

"What scoundrels they all are!" jokes the officer; "one would think they had all entered into an agreement to jostle you or fall under your horse."

Iona looks round at the officer, and moves his lips. He evidently wants to say something, but the only sound that issues is a snuffle.

"What?" asks the officer.

Iona twists his mouth into a smile, and with an effort says hoarsely:

"My son, *barin,* died this week."

"Hm! What did he die of?"

Iona turns with his whole body toward his fare, and says:

"And who knows! They say high fever. He was three days in the hospital, and then died. . . . God's will be done."

"Turn round! The devil!" sounds from the darkness. "Have you popped off, old doggie, eh? Use your eyes!"

"Go on, go on," says the officer, "otherwise we shall not get there by tomorrow. Hurry up a bit!"

The cabdriver again stretches his neck, sits up, and, with a bad grace, brandishes his whip. Several times again he turns to look at his fare, but the latter has closed his eyes, and apparently is not disposed to listen. Having deposited the officer in the Viborg, he stops by the tavern, doubles himself up on his seat, and again remains motionless, while the snow once more begins to cover him and his horse. An hour, and another. . . . Then, along the footpath, with a squeak of galoshes, and quarreling, come three young men, two of them tall and lanky, the third one short and hump-backed.

"Cabby, to the Police Bridge!" in a cracked voice calls the humpback. "The three of us for two *griveniks!*"

Iona picks up his reins, and smacks his lips. Two *griveniks* is not a fair price, but he does not mind whether it is a *rouble* or five *kopeks*—to him it is all the same now, so long as they are fares. The young men, jostling each other and using bad language, approach the sleigh, and all three at once try to get onto the seat; then begins a discussion as to which two shall sit and who shall be the one to stand. After wrangling, abusing each other, and much petulance, it is at last decided that the humpback shall stand, as he is the smallest.

"Now then, hurry up!" says the humpback in a twanging voice, as he takes his place and breathes in Iona's neck. "Old furry! Here, mate, what a cap you have! There is not a worse one to be found in all Petersburg! . . ."

"He-he!—he-he!" giggles Iona. "Such a . . ."

"Now you, 'such a,' hurry up, are you going the whole way at this pace? Are you? . . . Do you want it in the neck?"

"My head feels like bursting," says one of the lanky ones. "Last night at the Donkmasovs, Vaska and I drank the whole of four bottles of cognac."

"I don't understand what you lie for," says the other lanky one angrily; "you lie like a brute."

"God strike me, it's the truth!"

"It's as much the truth as that a louse coughs!"

"He, he," grins Iona, "what gay young gentlemen!"

"Pshaw, go to the devil!" says the humpback indignantly.

"Are you going to get on or not, you old pest? Is that the way to drive? Use the whip a bit! Go on, devil, go on, give it to him well!"

Iona feels at his back the little man wriggling, and the trem-
ble in his voice. He listens to the insults hurled at him, sees the
people, and little by little the feeling of loneliness leaves him.
The humpback goes on swearing until he gets mixed up in some
elaborate six-foot oath, or chokes with coughing. The lankies
begin to talk about a certain Nadejda Petrovna. Iona looks
round at them several times; he waits for a temporary silence,
then, turning round again, he murmurs:

"My son . . . died this week."

"We must all die," sighs the humpback, wiping his lips after
an attack of coughing. "Now, hurry up, hurry up! Gentlemen,
I really cannot go any farther like this! When will he get us
there?"

"Well, just you stimulate him a little in the neck!"

"You old pest, do you hear, I'll bone your neck for you! If
one treated the like of you with ceremony one would have to
go on foot! Do you hear, old serpent Gorinytch! Or do you not
care a spit?"

Iona hears rather than feels the blows they deal him.

"He, he," he laughs. "They are gay young gentlemen, God
bless 'em!"

"Cabby, are you married?" asks a lanky one.

"I? He, he, gay young gentlemen! Now I have only a wife
and the moist ground. . . . He, ho, ho . . . that is to say, the
grave. My son has died, and I am alive. . . . A wonderful
thing, death mistook the door . . . instead of coming to me, it
went to my son. . . ."

Iona turns round to tell them how his son died, but at this
moment, the humpback, giving a little sigh, announces, "Thank
God, we have at last reached our destination," and Iona watches
them disappear through the dark entrance. Once more he is
alone, and again surrounded by silence. . . . His grief, which
has abated for a short while, returns and rends his heart with
greater force. With an anxious and hurried look, he searches
among the crowds passing on either side of the street to find
whether there may be just one person who will listen to him.
But the crowds hurry by without noticing him or his trouble.

Yet it is such an immense, illimitable grief. Should his heart break and the grief pour out, it would flow over the whole earth, so it seems, and yet no one sees it. It has managed to conceal itself in such an insignificant shell that no one can see it even by day and with a light.

Iona sees a hall porter with some sacking, and decides to talk to him.

"Friend, what sort of time is it?" he asks.

"Past nine. What are you standing here for? Move on."

Iona moves on a few steps, doubles himself up, and abandons himself to his grief. He sees it is useless to turn to people for help. In less than five minutes he straightens himself, holds up his head as if he felt some sharp pain, and gives a tug at the reins; he can bear it no longer. "The stables," he thinks, and the little horse, as if it understood, starts off at a trot.

About an hour and a half later Iona is seated by a large dirty stove. Around the stove, on the floor, on the benches, people are snoring; the air is thick and suffocatingly hot. Iona looks at the sleepers, scratches himself, and regrets having returned so early.

"I have not even earned my fodder," he thinks. "That's what's my trouble. A man who knows his job, who has had enough to eat, and his horse too, can always sleep peacefully."

A young cabdriver in one of the corners half gets up, grunts sleepily, and stretches towards a bucket of water.

"Do you want a drink?" Iona asks him.

"Don't I want a drink!"

"That's so? Your good health! But listen, mate—you know, my son is dead. . . . Did you hear? This week, in the hospital. . . . It's a long story."

Iona looks to see what effect his words have, but sees none— the young man has hidden his face and is fast asleep again. The old man sighs, and scratches his head. Just as much as the young one wants to drink, the old man wants to talk. It will soon be a week since his son died, and he has not been able to speak about it properly to anyone. One must tell it slowly and carefully; how his son fell ill, how he suffered, what he said before he died, how he died. One must describe every detail of the funeral, and the journey to the hospital to fetch the dead son's clothes. His daughter Anissia has remained in the village—one must talk about her too. Is it nothing he has to tell? Surely the listener would gasp and sigh, and sympathize with him? It is better, too, to talk to women; although they are stupid, two words are enough to make them sob.

"I'll go and look after my horse," thinks Iona; "there's always time to sleep. No fear of that!"

He puts on his coat, and goes to the stables to his horse; he thinks of the corn, the hay, the weather. When he is alone, he dares not think of his son; he can speak about him to anyone, but to think of him, and picture him to himself, is unbearably painful.

"Are you tucking in?" Iona asks his horse, looking at its bright eyes; "go on, tuck in, though we've not earned our corn, we can eat hay. Yes! I am too old to drive—my son could have, not I. He was a first-rate cabdriver. If only he had lived!"

Iona is silent for a moment, then continues:

"That's how it is, my old horse. There's no more Kuzma Ionitch. He has left us to live, and he went off pop. Now let's say, you had a foal, you were the foal's mother, and suddenly, let's say, that foal went and left you to live after him. It would be sad, wouldn't it?"

The little horse munches, listens, and breathes over its master's hand. . . .

Iona's feelings are too much for him, and he tells the little horse the whole story.

XIII

The Talented Student

As every teacher knows, all students are not created equal. And they are not created equal in rights since those who demonstrate zeal—like those who have talent—deserve more attention than the others, after a time. Provided that they have average intelligence and no pressing personal problems, all students can be taught to write; they can be shown the elements of good writing and how to use them in a variety of forms. Yet, however, true it is (and it is true) that accomplishment rests mainly on effort, one or two or even three of your students will lead the rest, and these few should be started on a novel. In an exceptional class, all the students should begin a novel, but I am assuming that most classes of writing are not exceptional, and that even with the short story, two or three assignments may be necessary before each student has written a satisfactory one.

It will probably come about that your talented students themselves will want to try a novel and will suggest it to you. To tell them that they should do so in a more advanced writing class—which they may not be able to afford later or might attend only after the first fires of their enthusiasm have vanished—is to do them a disservice. And an equal disservice is to give them a long reading list of great novels with the assumption that they can be inspired by quantity. They might find, on the contrary, that after reading a dozen "great" novels their confidence is drowned. And the common objections that a novel cannot be written by anyone without "experience of life," or that someone over fifty who has never written anything (and who uses bad grammar) is an utter fool to attempt a novel unless he serves a long apprenticeship, are objections which are not only cynical but easily overthrown.

It is a good idea to announce to the class that you will hold office hours to interview anyone who has a novel in mind. There will be some students for whom the interview (talking it over, then helping them settle on a plot outline and deciding on major and minor characters who will experience the theme) will be the first step. There will be others whose novel really is only a plan for a short story, and you will help them to write it. Of course, the students who do have an idea which can be made into a novel are not easily confused with those who do not. If the former have a set of characters, and not merely one or two; if they have a plot which will allow their characters to move about in a variety of settings; if they have a theme in mind which can be experienced by several of their characters, then they do have a novel and can begin to write its first chapter. And it is for these students that some reading of novels may be valuable, especially if the teacher knows of particular novels related to their projected ones. In addition, the reading of a few, near-perfect novels—although only a few—is likely to prove something of an inspiration. Such works of art as *Pride and Prejudice, All Quiet on the Western Front,* and Pär Lagerkvist's *The Sibyl* should not destroy confidence, although they might.

In general, the requirements of the first chapter of a novel are the same as those for the first paragraph or so of a short story. In the first chapter of a novel

1. The main character must be introduced although he need not be directly presented. He can be talked about, and he ought to be at least mentioned

2. The narrative focus must be clearly given and maintained throughout all subsequent chapters. (The oftnoted example of Virginia Woolf's *Orlando* as a contradiction of this rule is not a contradiction; she does not change the narrator, she changes his sex.)

3. The setting must be clear and by its tone ought to reflect the nature of the theme. (Dickens is especially good with this, but so are most major novelists.) Although settings change in a novel, as they do not in a short story, the most important setting must be indicated as such in the most important chapter, which is chapter one

4. Just enough of the conflict, the forces that make up the movement of character and action, should be given in chapter one to make the reader wonder "what will happen now?"; in short, the incidents should begin

And in regard to the novels mentioned above, it will be helpful if the students read at least the first chapter of each of them. All contain first chapters that are brilliantly successful examples of what first chapters should be.

When their first chapters are finished, ask the students to outline the remaining ones before the end of the semester. After all, your students may not take another writing class and, more important, a detailed, chapter-by-chapter outline will prevent the famous "writer's block"; it will give them a plan and a direction when their confidence and enthusiasm bog down.

Occasionally you will find a poet among your students. He will want, and deserve, special attention. Unfortunately, he will also expect that you will give him rules to follow in order to write successful poetry. And since there are no rules but only forms, like the Ode, the Elizabethan and Petrarchan sonnet, the epic, etc., it will be difficult indeed for you to help him. In my years of writing classes, I have come upon only one student who was really a poet. Two others wanted to become poets, and I suggested what books I knew, such as Brooks and Warren's *Understanding Poetry* and Pound's *ABC of Reading*, but they did not produce poetry, at least during the time they were my students.

Magazine articles are a different matter. Here you can be very helpful indeed. Although, as in the short story and the novel, the writer writes from his own experience and knowledge, he must pay far more attention than the fiction writer to accuracy and clarity. The five questions of journalism— Who, What, When, Where, and Why—will be important to him, and he must "aim" his article, even before he writes it, even in the planning stage, at a magazine which publishes articles of the same kind as his projected one. An article, for example, which might be published in the *Saturday Evening Post* will never be published in *Harper's* magazine. And it will not be published in the *Saturday Evening Post* either unless it fits the form of that magazine's already published articles.

There is a book that will be more than helpful here. It is called *The Writer's Market* and can be found in any large library. It is a kind of telephone book for publishing and lists every periodical published in the United States with addresses, the names of their fiction and nonfiction editors, and a brief description of the kind of material they publish and are likely to buy. This, of course, is not a substitute for the writer's familiarity with the particular magazine he is writing for, but it is useful and it is the place to find other magazines likely to accept his manuscript.

Children's books and stories represent a fertile field. Indeed, teenage fiction, as published, for example, in such American magazines as *Seventeen, Co-Ed,* and *Practical English*, may be the best kind of fiction for younger student writers to attempt. Also, there are textbooks for writers who aim at the teenage market. Some of these do tell the writer how to arrange the elements of his articles or stories in order to please his special audience. But the elements of a story for teenagers are the same as those of a story for adults. Those writers I have known who have been successful with children's literature are, simply, successful writers. The only startling difference between the adult and nonadult fiction markets is that the latter almost exactly mirrors, in its subject matter, the current, popular, man-in-the-street thinking about the issues of the day. At the moment, children's and teenagers' books and stories with racial integration as their subjects are almost sure to sell, provided, of course, that they are sympathetic and well done. But the fashions change.

A last word here about what might be called the "Late Arriver." He is, or will prove to be, one of your talented students. But he is also the young man or woman (or older man or woman) who has produced tearjerking excuses throughout most of the semester. Indeed, he may have caught your fancy by the very elaboration of detail in the excuses. However, by midterm you will have consigned him to the handful of dropouts—with the concession, of course, that he seems to lack the character even to decide to drop out. You may have decided that he is simply a Lost Cause.

But he is not. Somewhere after the mid-semester and when it is patently too late to change his "F" final grade into a "B" or an "A," he will begin to write. The writing will be bad, and you will have to arrange for more than just a few interviews in order to tell him, over his papers, what you have already told him and the class about the papers weeks before. But he will improve. At the end of the semester he will have improved enough to plunge you into the dilemma of giving him the "F" you had planned or the "Incomplete" which most universities and colleges permit. (He will usually have elaborate reasons as to why you should give him an "Incomplete.") However, a small act of faith is useful here. He will be willing, nay, eager, to mail you his assignments; a surprising number of Late Arrivers become entirely dependable and zealous correspondents. Throughout the second term or during your summer holiday, you will be reading his late papers while incredulously shaking your head.

But this Late Arriver may develop into the most promising young writer of the class.

XIV

Variations and Theme

If the art of teaching is, as it is, somewhat different from any other art, it may be because the roles of the teacher are multiple. And not the least of his roles is that of master of ceremonies. The teacher works with his students to encourage, enlighten, educate, and inspire them. But he, above all, must keep them interested. A visit to the classroom by a published writer (whether he has published novels, children's books, short stories, or poems in an American seed catalogue) is a variation on even eloquent lectures. Sometimes such a visit, and such a visitor, is an inspiration to the students. Nearly always, it is interesting.

These writers can be found often within the college faculty. If this fails, the usual small-town librarian will know of one or two, and a well-worded invitation from you as teacher may get a possibly lonely writer into your classroom with benefit to all concerned. In a sense, it hardly matters what the writer says once he is in the classroom; the students will ask questions, and it is the fact of his publications that you wish to emphasize, in any case.

In New York City, Chicago, San Francisco, and other big American cities, there are dozens of "readings" where published poets and novelists read their works aloud. These can be attended by the class as a whole or by the students individually, and nearly always they are valuable. (I remember taking a class to hear Allen Ginsberg, whom they did not like but who inspired them just the same—in spite of themselves.) Also, impossible though it may seem, movies made from short stories or novels which the class has read and discussed are extremely valuable, if strange, assignments.

There are other variations, other ways to stimulate good writing. Many of the major poets and novelists who write in English have made recordings of their work. A recording of Vachel Lindsay reading his famous poem "The Congo" is, for example, the most effective device I have used to stimulate a "slow" class. Such poets as Dylan Thomas and T. S. Eliot are represented by several record albums easily obtained from college or public libraries. James Joyce has himself recorded passages from *Ulysses,* and whole plays by Shakespeare have been "done" in recordings by excellent actors. The effect upon the class will be, of course, an emphasis upon words and their weight and variations and values.

Other devices depend on paraphernalia from the college library which usually contains such things as overhead projectors and opaque projectors for use in all kinds of ways. With them, a page of student writing can be projected on a screen and corrected, by you, while the class watches—and, one hopes, learns. A page from a published novel or short story can be analyzed in this way, and the importance of cutting can be made extremely clear by these means.

Also valuable are field trips, interviews, and attics.

It is interesting occasionally to take the class outside the classroom—perhaps to a Buddhist church (there are several in New York and Chicago), a loading pier, where it is often possible to go aboard the freighters, or even a train depot (Noël Coward did much with this not-at-all-mundane setting in his play *Brief Encounter*). On these trips the class can take notes and compare them later in the classroom. Perhaps the notes will serve as setting for a short story; ideas for plot or theme or characterization come quickly when one of the elements of fiction, such as setting, has been decided upon. And such a trip will unify the group, as common endeavors usually do.

And since writers base the majority of their characters on real people, an interview with almost anyone of interest can do two things at once: it can stimulate the student to write and it can also provide him with material to write from. Within the college community itself there are myriad examples of travels to foreign lands and consequent strange adventures, publications and stories of how the publications were achieved, and experiences in war. (Some years ago a student's interview with an uncle who had fought in the Irish Rising of 1916 resulted in a characterization which later became an interesting, and published, short story. The student had known of the uncle's experience, but it was the interview itself that turned the experience into material for fiction.)

Attics also are sometimes mother lodes. A humpbacked trunk, besides revealing a yellowed wedding dress or photograph album, will occasionally contain a diary, journal, or long-forgotten newspaper clipping—perhaps even a long-forgotten manuscript. The urge to write is not confined to one generation.

Big-city living of course precludes attics. But big-city bureau drawers sometimes hold forgotten appointment books, dance programs, or a carefully folded Army uniform. Any and all of these can be beginnings.

Theme

Since theme is the element of fiction which the class will find the most difficult to understand and use, an added hour or two devoted to the analysis of theme (taken perhaps from a thoughtful editorial in the local paper) will be useful and, in fact, sometimes necessary. And an analysis of the elements of a novel assigned as outside reading will be the most useful of all. Here I recommend *A Farewell to Arms* because its clear statement of theme, both by the hero and by minor characters, and its symbols illustrating theme (the rain, autumn, the falling leaves) will help the class immeasurably. Another novel written with equal clarity and equally useful to demonstrate theme is John Steinbeck's *Grapes of Wrath*. As in *A Farewell to Arms,* its title, chief characters (Tom and Ma Joad, and the preacher) , and symbols (the turtle, the two camps, and the deaths of the grandparents) , all reflect its themes in ways the class can discover and learn from.

However, even if the teacher is unwilling to burden his students with reading assignments, the importance of theme in both fiction and nonfiction should be stressed. And with it the logic of an idea which is theme. American students are rarely trained to think, and the American way of life seems to leave less and less room for thoughtful conversation. The widespread and effective media of communication which bombard the American with news stories and speeches and, on TV, movies interrupted by almost constant commercials, seem to dull the viewer and listener rather than stimulate him. As every American teacher knows, the problem he has is not in presenting his material to the students but in making them want it.

That a theme is a complete idea that should be verbalized or written out *before* it is used in any form of writing is a fact worth perhaps stronger emphasis on the part of the teacher than any other. When it is understood by the students, it will make the difference between papers which say something and those which don't. Any methods the teacher can invent to help his students use theme well are going to be of value.

XV

The Long Paper;
Publication; Failures

The students should hand in their research cards about two weeks after you've assigned them, their outlines a week or so later, and their long research papers several weeks before the end of the semester, since some will have to be rewritten.

To accept a paper which should be unacceptable is to do the student a major disservice. Probably he will not have another opportunity to write a research paper under supervision and in steps as this was written. If the paper, therefore, lacks a bibliography or footnote page, if it is a mass of quotations without quotation marks, or if it abounds in puerile errors of spelling or punctuation, it should be returned to the student to be corrected and changed. For the value of excellence is learned perhaps only in its pursuit. It is possible that some of your students will have passed through their years of education entirely without challenge to their minds or interests. They may have developed habits of *un*excellence or feel that their capacities are limited because they have never really used them. Permissiveness has reached dangerous proportions in some areas of American life, and rules have become almost an anachronism—but you need not apologize to your students for making them.

It is wise to read the long papers carefully. Often they turn out to be better than the teacher expects; one or two of them, sometimes, turn out to be really publishable. In writing classes, as in other kinds of classes within the university, the student will produce in direct ratio to the teacher's demands, and if his reach exceeds his grasp, he will nevertheless reach toward a mark only as high as you have set for him.

Besides the invaluable *Writer's Market* already mentioned, the writing teacher should become familiar with the many small magazines that publish student material. Some of these are also listed in the *Reader's Guide to Periodical Literature,* and they are very good places to send student work, especially the long research paper.

Writing contests of all kinds are important to know about and to suggest to students who may want to enter them; even the experience of preparing a manuscript for possible publication will be an incentive. Scholastic Magazines' annual short story contest, for example, like that of *Mademoiselle* and others, insists that all material submitted be written by students. Also, the standards used in these contests are generally somewhat lower than those used by fiction editors of adult magazines. The point is that students are reluctant to submit manuscripts for publication. They need prodding to do so. And there is no greater incentive for them to continue writing, once the semester is finished and the class ended, than publication.

There are certain minor requirements for the submission of manuscripts which you might tell your students about—although the most important requirement of all, once the story or essay has been finally honed and polished, is that it be sent to a periodical which has already published similar work.

The manuscript should be prepared carefully. An editor is only a human being and is much more likely to look with favor upon a neat manuscript than an illegible one, even if the second contains sparks of real genius. Also, he is much more likely to send the author of the first a friendly letter to soften the enclosed rejection slip.

The manuscript should

1. be a perfect copy without corrections, erasures, or typing errors
2. be typed on unlined, regulation typing paper, and double-spaced
3. contain the title, author's name and address, and the approximate wordage at the top of the first page
4. be numbered in the upper right-hand corners
5. be mailed in a stamped, self-addressed, manila envelope, with another stamped, self-addressed, manila envelope enclosed to ensure its return

And the student should absolutely reject the temptation to write a letter of inquiry when weeks pass with no word from the editor. Such letters usually are ignored anyway.

Certainly one of the responsibilities of a teacher of writing is to provide encouragement, but this is especially true when rejection slips are interpreted by students, as they usually are, as being signs of failure. Here a fascinating, largely autobiographical novel, Jack London's *Martin Eden,* could be recommended outside reading. The book dramatizes more completely than any teacher could do the loneliness of the writer and the necessity for his stubborn perserverance. It also describes what happens to earlier rejected manuscripts when a later one is accepted, for once a writer has "broken through," all of his work will be read with interest.

But the teacher can smooth the way of the student writer by other means. He can suggest markets, including the college literary magazines; he can be helpful when letters-from-the-editors do come and point up a persistent writing fault; and he can feel enough concern for his students to give them his summer address—for future manuscripts and future encouragement.

Failures

About which a decision must be made in relation to a fundamental question: Is it the teacher's fault or the student's? Why *didn't* he write?

Recent studies of job failures indicate that the reasons given, such as absenteeism, failure to achieve work standards, personality conflicts, indicate that the worker was suffering not from being a square peg in a round hole, from failure to measure up, but was rather insufficiently motivated. And "insufficiently motivated" means, according to these surveys, that the employee was treated like a machine, that no one clucked over him, no one drew him out, no one offered help when the inevitable problems and blocks occurred.

This may be the case of your student, or students, who did not write.

No one is at the same time educator, mother hen, psychiatrist, critic, and master of ceremonies except the teacher. (If this seems fulsome or outrageously sentimental, try to remember some of your own "good" teachers and their importance to you.) The interview, which so often begins with a discussion of the student's work and ends with a recitation of his dilemmas or frustrations, is the place for clucking. In the case of the poor student, you may not have clucked enough. Perhaps the failure is really a well-disguised Late Arriver and needs only another interview to really begin to write. Perhaps the failure *is,* after all, your own. . . .

The student who has not tried presents to every teacher the problem of when to give up and whether or not he should give up.

But the answer to this problem is largely unknown.

XVI

Last Chores

During the last class sessions the writers' notebooks should be collected, graded, and returned. They will be amazingly varied—a few desultory pages or an accomplished manuscript made up of many forms of writing. They are important because they may help to decide upon a final grade, but also, like all the assignments, they will reflect the student's talent and zeal. Sometimes they will require interviews—when a particular entry is promising, for example, and should be developed more fully, or when an entry indicates that the student is not completely clear about a writing form.

The question of a final examination, too, should be discussed with the students. Most universities and colleges allow the writing instructor to decide for himself whether or not he will give a final. To me it has seemed always a redundancy. The students throughout the semester have written enough.

But there is time in a last class session for you to talk about writing as something which the students can continue to do. The faces of a last class are, unlike those of the first class, generally faces of friends. To a teacher of writing, the inner lives of his students are generally quite well known by the time the last interview has been given and the last paper returned. The aspirations and hopes, the limitations and fears, of your students may have been made so clear that you will find it prudent to discount more than you remember when you think of them afterwards. A human being becomes; he is in a perpetual state of change. And your comments on their papers, like the final grades you have given them, are not and cannot be the final evaluation of either what they can accomplish or what they will accomplish. And you should tell them this.

A final selection I have found most helpful to read aloud is the first page of James Agee's *A Death in the Family*. This is good, indeed it is almost great, writing and contains the elements of good writing in rather marvelous ways. (It can be used, also, to begin the semester, but I prefer to read it at the last class session.) In essence, the passage will emphasize to your students what they have of common experience, experience perhaps very similar to Agee's, which they, too, can write about and turn into short stories or novels. The point is that whether they will do so or not is partly up to you.